Assessment of the Consolidation of the Australian Customs and Border Protection Service (ACBPS) with the Department of Immigration and Border Protection (DIBP)

Daniel M. Gerstein, Karen Edwards, Dulani Woods, Julie Newell, Jennifer D. P. Moroney

For more information on this publication, visit www.rand.org/t/RR1713

Library of Congress Cataloging-in-Publication Data is available for this publication.
ISBN: 978-0-8330-9661-6

Published by the RAND Corporation, Santa Monica, Calif., under license.

Preface

On 7 May 2014, the Australian government announced the integration of the Australian Customs and Border Protection Service and the Department of Immigration and Border Protection (DIBP) into a single government department, including the formation of the Australian Border Force (ABF), by 1 July 2015.

A year after the integration began, the DIBP leadership sought an independent analysis of the effectiveness and efficiency of the integrated department. This analysis required the RAND Corporation to take a deeper and longer view of the two organisations as they existed, understand how the combined organisation has been able to incorporate into a single entity, and assess the degree to which the new organisation has been able to mitigate weaknesses and reinforce strengths.

RAND undertook a review of relevant documents and interviews with senior leaders from across the department, including the ABF. This report details the findings of this research. Numerous official documents, reports, and investigations dating back to 2005 documented the shortfalls and provided insights and recommendations for improving the respective organisations.

The case for change was clear going back to the earliest documents that were reviewed. The need for reform had been recognised in the earliest documents, from 2005. Some reforms had been implemented in a piecemeal fashion over the period from 2005 to 2015. However, these earlier efforts largely were designed to address specific shortfalls, not necessarily to build capacity and professionalise the organisations. Therefore, despite long and proud histories, neither organisation had developed the capabilities nor professionalisation in the workforce expected of a modern border-management organisation.

In looking at the case for change, the analysis focused on five areas in particular: (1) intelligence, (2) investigations, (3) detention, (4) integrity and corruption, and (5) learning and development. Performance as measured through the documents and interviews highlighted systemic shortfalls that contributed to, at best, consistent marginal performance and, at times, highly visible miscues that resulted in a loss of confidence by the public.

With the integration and subsequent reform, the DIBP is seeking to build a 21st-century border-management system able to respond to the increasing demands of the customs, immigration, and border-security subsystems. This activity has been ongoing for slightly over a year.

This study was sponsored by the DIBP, led by Secretary Michael Pezzullo and Australian Border Force Commissioner Roman Quaedvlieg, APM. The DIBP's Office of the First Assistant Secretary, Strategic Policy and Planning Division, served as the primary interlocutors with the RAND study team and provided support to the study effort. This research was conducted by researchers within RAND Australia; RAND Justice, Infrastructure, and Environment; and the RAND National Security Research Division.

Questions or comments about this report should be sent to the project leader, Daniel Gerstein (Daniel_Gerstein@rand.org). For questions regarding RAND Australia, please contact RAND Australia director Jennifer Moroney at moroney@rand.org or 61 2 6243 4869.

Contents

Figures and Tables

Figures

Tables

Summary

Background

On 7 May 2014, the government of Australia announced the integration of the Australian Customs and Border Protection Service (ACBPS) and the Department of Immigration and Border Protection (DIBP) into a single government department, including the formation of the Australian Border Force (ABF), by 1 July 2015.[1]

A year after the integration began, the DIBP leadership sought an independent analysis of the effectiveness and efficiency of the integrated department. This analysis required RAND to take a deeper and longer view of the two organisations as they existed, understand how the combined organisation has been able to incorporate into a single entity, and assess the degree to which the new organisation has been able to mitigate weaknesses and reinforce strengths.

Key Findings

The analysis suggests a number of key findings in four areas: (1) the case for change, (2) building a single border-management organisation, (3) assessing progress and performance, and (4) looking towards the future.

The Case for Change

- Systemic shortfalls in both the Customs and Immigration organisations, punctuated by several high-profile failings, were noted in the decade prior to the integration.

[1] The DIBP has undergone a number of name changes since 2001. From 2001 to 2006, it was called the Department of Immigration and Multicultural and Indigenous Affairs (DIMIA). From 2006 to 2007, it was the Department of Immigration and Multicultural Affairs (DIMA). From 2007 to 2013, it was called the Department of Immigration and Citizenship (DIAC). It became the DIBP in 2013; in July 2015, the ACBPS was integrated into a single department, called the DIBP. For the purpose of this report, *Immigration* will be used to refer to the pre-integration DIBP and its antecedents, while *Customs* will refer to the ACBPS. For the post-integration period (i.e., after July 2015), the organisation will be referred to as the DIBP.

  - Despite two high-profile, unlawful detention cases, which occurred in 2005, Immigration had not developed adequate control mechanisms to reduce the risk of future systemic failures of process.
  - The Immigration information technology (IT) solution "Systems for People" had failed to fully deliver on promised system reforms.
  - Customs had a very high-profile corruption case at Sydney Airport, first identified in 2007, that resulted in the conviction of three of the eight officers arrested. As a result, Customs had commenced implementation of integrity measures prior to the integration.
  - Both organisations had been cited for the lack of accountability amongst senior leaders.
- Despite long and proud histories, neither organisation had adequately developed the capabilities or professionalisation in the workforce expected of a modern border-management organisation.
  - Numerous official documents, reports, and investigations dating back to 2005 documented the shortfalls and provided insights and recommendations for improving the respective organisations.
  - Shortfalls were observed across each of the five areas that were examined in depth (i.e., intelligence, investigations, detention, integrity and corruption, and learning and development).
  - Many changes were implemented based on the numerous report findings. Yet these changes were not undertaken in a comprehensive manner; rather, they only addressed the noted shortfalls.
- Analysis indicates (particularly from interviews with senior leaders) that both organisations had perceived difficulty in collaborating and sharing information with each other and more broadly across the Australian government.

Building a Single Border-Management Organisation

- The transformation of Customs and Immigration would have been required to address the observed shortfalls regardless of the integration. The need for this transformation has been particularly drawn out through the Australian Public Service Commission capability reviews of the two organisations in 2012 and 2013.
- The 2013 National Commission of Audit recommended the merger of Customs and Immigration into a single organisation.
  - Previously, in a December 2008 National Security Statement, then–Prime Minister Kevin Rudd announced that the Australian government would be augmenting, retasking, and renaming the Australian Customs Service to create the new ACBPS.

  - Recommendations of the Smith Review included initiatives on organised crime, border security, and science and innovation.[2] The primary goal was to better coordinate overall national security arrangements.
- The integration represents an inflection point in the history of Australia's customs, immigration, and border-management activities.
- Planning for the integration began immediately after the Commission of Audit recommendation was approved—a comprehensive effort was developed for executing the transformation.
- Formal integration based on a well-developed, top-down–driven plan began on 1 July 2015.
- While planning for the 1 July 2015 integration was clearly evident, the necessary structures for assessing the integration—including time-phased goals and objectives, strategic and operational metrics, and leadership direction—were not in place or lacked maturity.

Assessing Progress and Performance

- Despite the turbulence of the integration and the reform effort, reduced resources, and increased operational tempo, the DIBP saw overall positive trends in performance during the period from 2014 to 2016.
  - This trend of doing more with less suggests that there were substantial efficiency gains and points to a positive fiscal dividend being delivered by the integrated organisation.
  - Overall, integration has served as a catalyst for increasing operational effectiveness and efficiency, as well as achieving much-needed change.
- Several noteworthy programs were included almost immediately to send a strong signal to the workforce and the public concerning the changes under way.
  - Examples of changes include transitioning to a single uniform for the Australian Border Force; standing up the Australian Border Force College; combining human resources and financial systems; and integrating the communications, media, and parliamentary functions.
- Shortly after the integration formally began, during the early phase of execution, there were difficulties with a loss of momentum regarding the reorganisation.
- Corrective measures were implemented, including developing new metrics for assessing operational effectiveness and efficiency.
  - Particularly since March 2016, there has been a greater emphasis on building the foundational capacity needed for the long-term professionalisation of the newly formed DIBP.

---

[2] Anthony Bergin, *A Safer Australia: Meeting the Challenges of Homeland Security*, Barton: Australian Strategic Policy Institute, 30 January 2009.

- The announced one-year timeline for integration was unrealistic; in many areas, the newly formed DIBP remains in the early stages of reform—an example is building a single DIBP culture, which will take much longer to achieve.

Looking Towards the Future

- More effort on capacity-building is required across the department; leadership visibility will be required to ensure continued momentum.
- Building a single DIBP culture (including workforce morale and professionalisation) remains the single biggest challenge for the DIBP.
- The formation of the Strategic Reform Group under the leadership of the deputy secretary both established the responsibility for the coordination of integration efforts and sent an important message to the workforce about the priority of the integration.
- According to several senior officials who were interviewed, achieving the full reform is at least three to five years away. Some officials commented that it could take a generation until the comprehensive change envisioned by the DIBP leadership is realised.

Specific Findings: The Case for Change

A review of documents and content from interviews with senior leaders from across the department, including the ABF, demonstrates the leadership's commitment towards the integration to ensure that a more operationally effective and efficient organisation will be created.

The need for reform had been recognised in the earliest documents from 2005, which were provided to the RAND team. Some reforms had been implemented in a piecemeal fashion over the period from 2005 to 2015. However, these earlier efforts largely were designed to address specific shortfalls but not necessarily to build capacity and professionalise the organisations.

For this study, five areas were directed by DIBP to be the focus of the analysis: (1) intelligence, (2) investigations, (3) detention, (4) integrity and corruption, and (5) learning and development. Some of the more-noteworthy shortfalls across the five areas have been consolidated in Table S.1.

Specific Findings: Operational Effectiveness

In assessing operational effectiveness, RAND was asked to evaluate the effectiveness of this newly formed department by examining the data from the period of 2014–2016. This analysis focused on developing quantitatively informed trends.

Table S.1
The Case for Change

Category	Assessment: The Case for Change (Pre-Integration)
General findings	• Despite long and proud histories, both organisations lacked consistent professionalism and standards in executing their responsibilities across the workforce • Both organisations had observed difficulties working with each other and across the government • There was little indication of focus on accountability in either of the two organisations • Both organisations had strong, entrenched cultures • While the rationale for the integration was understood by the senior leadership, many in the workforce were not convinced of the need for the reorganisation • Lack of holistic management of the border noted by several senior people during interviews
Intelligence	• Neither organisation did well in consistently sharing intelligence with each other or across the government • Organisationally, Customs had a division that primarily focused on tactical intelligence, while Immigration only had a small team with limited maturity looking for noncompliance with the *Migration Act 1958* and illegal maritime arrival screening rather than national security concerns • Neither organisation had the capacity to support their organisations with standard (repeatable) intelligence products
Investigations	• Prior to the reorganisation, there was not enough emphasis on employing proper rules and procedures • There was not enough emphasis on educating the workforce about integrity and anticorruption issues • There was no cross-training of officers across all functions of the Immigration or Customs agencies
Detention	• For the former Department of Immigration, several high-profile issues were noted regarding detention, including child-protection concerns • There was a very large backlog of illegal maritime arrival cases and a lack of evident operational and fiscal discipline • Management of onshore detention was outsourced, resulting in inadequate immigration control and accountability over detention operations
Integrity and corruption	• Noted problems with corruption meant that Customs had been working, pre-integration, to address this issue; Immigration had never formally identified issues of this kind • Customs conducted an internal vetting process prior to 2010; universal standards for vetting of officers were developed in October 2010; for Immigration, the requirement for all officers to acquire a minimum of baseline security clearance through the Australian Government Security Vetting Agency was not universally enforced • There was no standardised training and development programs for integrity and corruption
Learning and development	• Few systemic foundations for learning and development had been established in either organisation prior to the integration; what did exist in Immigration was limited in scope and certainly not comprehensive • No concept for cross-training or professionalisation existed prior to integration • Attempts to improve the workforce were largely undertaken to address specific deficiencies and not as part of systemic professionalisation of the workforce

Two overarching themes during this period were the increased operational tempo and the ongoing integration. Throughout, the DIBP has supported the government of Australia in the customs, immigration, and border-protection mission following the integration with no observable decrease in capability while undergoing a significant reorganisation and a decrease in top-line funding. RAND examined 130 operational programme performance measures. The results indicate that 64 measures (49 percent) met targets or were improving, 29 (22 percent) remained constant, 15 (12 percent) did not meet targets or were declining, and 22 (17 percent) could not be determined (i.e., the data were either not available or the trends were not identifiable). Table S.2 lists the categories of the measures and their assessments.

Table S.2
Operational Effectiveness Assessment

Category	Description	Assessment
Operational effectiveness and efficiency	Support for the customs, immigration, and border mission (i.e., operational tempo)	• No observed loss in effectiveness across operational missions • Increases in trade and travel were noted during the period • Given reductions in the budget, there has been an increase in efficiency: More than 70 percent of the operational metrics show improvement or have remained constant
Culture and personnel	Indicators of the effects on the culture of DIBP and personnel programs	• Strong indications of support for workforce and attempts to build a common DIBP culture • Strong leadership commitment, yet recent employee survey showed negative views concerning several key metrics, including perceptions of senior leadership • Unforeseen challenges identified in interviews regarding combining two entrenched organisations, including disparities in pay and concern about working conditions
Capability	Programs and process designed to build organisational capacity	• Little direct quantitative evidence of capability-building, yet important qualitative evidence (e.g., common human resources and financial systems, ABF College development)
Action plan for reorganisation	Examination of the reorganisation planning for pre- and postexecution	• Strong preexecution plan developed, but shortfalls noted in post-integration period (i.e., did not contain adequate metrics that were defined and measurable and also included assumptions and thresholds)
Monitoring progress of reorganisation	Capabilities for monitoring the progress of the reorganisation	• Shortfalls noted in the monitoring of the integration (e.g., leadership visibility of progress, inadequate metrics to track progress [at both the strategic and operational levels], desire for greater communication with workforce)

Additional Findings

During the review of documents, interviews, and analysis, several overarching conclusions were developed.

First, a terminology issue surfaced during the course of the interviews and review of documents. Three terms were used somewhat interchangeably throughout these sources: *integration*, *reorganisation*, and *reform*. *Integration* and *reorganisation* predominantly refer to the period beginning with the 2013 Commission of Audit and ending with 1 July 2016, which was a year after the integration officially began. *Reform* entails a broader concept of organisational capability-building and professionalisation of the workforce. However, the delineation of these terms was not universally understood.

In many respects, the view of integration looks different when viewing the issue from either the top down or bottom up. Those inside the ABF involved in operations believed that the integration will continue to occur over the next three to five years and must include elements that could be considered organisational reform. At the DIBP headquarters, the senior leaders understood the messaging that integration was complete as of 1 July 2016, and subsequent efforts will be characterised as reform.

However, discussions indicated that many believed that the one-year period for achieving integration was too ambitious. Therefore, despite the messaging, analysis suggests that some integration efforts will still be ongoing after the one-year period allotted for integration. One example is the integration of the IT systems. Another issue that remains a work in progress is documenting the roles and authorities of the cross-functional teams; several interviewees remarked that team members were still learning how to function in this new integrated environment.

Second, the cultural aspects of the integration cannot be overstated. Discussions with senior leaders from across the DIBP indicated that they observed a slowly changing climate within the broader workforce. Many came to see the value of the integration and the subsequent reform, yet some still felt a sense of loss of identity relating to the integration. Some who did not see the value of the integration left the department for other positions in the government or chose to leave government altogether. In terms of workforce acceptance of the integration, a consistent characterisation in the senior-leader interviews was that 30 percent of staff were appreciative of the change, 50 percent remained on the fence, and 20 percent remained resistant to the change.

Exacerbating the cultural divide are core issues relating to the workforce. Tensions exist regarding such workforce issues as remuneration and promotions. Systemic differences that had existed prior to 1 July 2015 continue to be a source of friction despite attempts as part of the integration to normalise these differences.

Furthermore, while operational efficiency and professionalisation efforts have continued, personal loyalties to the former organisations exist and will likely continue for some time. Branding activities (such as a common uniform for all ABF officers) and celebrating or recognising organisational success will serve to minimise these issues over time.

Third, recruitment of senior leaders as part of the integration and reform has served to top load expertise and more rapidly professionalise important functions within the department. Examples include the intelligence and detention operations areas, where professionals from outside the DIBP were brought in to build the department's capacity in these areas.

Fourth, resource constraints appear to be well understood by senior leaders yet will need to be addressed for reform to continue. For example, technologies must be resourced and fielded before reductions in the top line are taken. In some cases, efficiencies were taken before systems were in place. Several senior leaders highlighted the need for resource investments for both workforce professionalisation and organisational technology capability development.

Fifth, departmental-level senior-leader engagement was seen as an imperative in continuing efforts to reform the DIBP. The need for continued reform following the completion of the one-year integration was also a recurrent theme; recognition exists that reaching the goals of the integration (and reform) will take another three to five years.

Conclusions

The integration of the former Customs and Immigration into the DIBP reflects an important inflection point in the history of customs, immigration, and border-management activities within the government of Australia.

With the integration of the DIBP formally beginning in July 2015, a comprehensive transformation had been clearly envisioned. And with the original integration period over the past 12 months completed, reform efforts to realise the full transformation are continuing. Given the leadership commitment and the capacity-building foundations being developed, such a comprehensive reform is possible.

The degree to which the integration and reform will achieve their goals largely rests on the ability of the leadership to keep up the momentum, bring the workforce along, develop a unified DIBP culture, and ensure that the capacities that have been built are able to survive.

Acknowledgements

This work benefited from the input and assistance of numerous people. Our study sponsor, the Department of Immigration and Border Protection (DIBP)—including Secretary Michael Pezzullo and Australian Border Force Commissioner Roman Quaedvlieg, APM—initiated this important introspective study effort. Further, the department allowed access to official documentation and senior leaders for interviews, which provided the study team understanding of the pre- and post-integration period. The Office of the First Assistant Secretary Strategic Policy and Planning within the DIBP served as the primary interlocutors with the RAND Corporation study team and provided outstanding support to the effort.

We also wish to thank the interviewees who candidly and generously shared their experiences and thoughts with the RAND team; their insights were essential to the conclusions reached in this report. The feedback from the DIBP reviewers was likewise invaluable to shaping the final report and ensuring accuracy in the judgments that were made.

Finally, we wish thank our administrative assistants, Cecile St. Julien and Marissa Robinson, and our management team, including Anita Chandra and Seth Jones, for their contributions to this effort. We are also appreciative of the comments from our reviewer, Henry Willis, and the RAND publication team that expertly supported the development of the final report.

CHAPTER ONE

Introduction

Study Objectives and Tasks

On 7 May 2014, the government of Australia announced the integration of the Australian Customs and Border Protection Service (ACBPS) and the Department of Immigration and Border Protection (DIBP) into a single government department, including the formation of the Australian Border Force (ABF), by 1 July 2015.[1]

The overarching study objective was to assess the degree to which the integration of the two organisations resulted in a more capable organisation, building on its perceived strengths while mitigating the weaknesses of the individual organisations.

Two distinct analyses were undertaken as part of this study effort. One looked at the case for change, identifying the rationale for transforming the Customs and Immigration organisations. The other examined the operational performance of the DIBP, including the progress of integration from the period 14 May 2014 to 14 May 2016.

Analysis of the Case for Change

In looking at the case for change, the study team conducted the analysis using a combination of research techniques. The research team was tasked with answering the following questions: What did the two organisations look like separately? What has been done in the integrated organisation to harness the strengths of both former agencies? What had been done to mitigate the weaknesses of the two former organisations?

---

[1] The DIBP has undergone a number of name changes since 2001. From 2001 to 2006, it was called the Department of Immigration and Multicultural and Indigenous Affairs. From 2006 to 2007, it was the Department of Immigration and Multicultural Affairs. From 2007 to 2013, it was called the Department of Immigration and Citizenship (DIAC). It became the DIBP in 2013; in July 2015, the ACBPS was integrated into a single department, called the DIBP. For the purpose of this report, *Immigration* will be used to refer to the pre-integration DIBP and its antecedents, while *Customs* will refer to the ACBPS. For the post-integration period, the organisation will be referred to as the DIBP. The terms *pre-* and *post-integration* refer to the point immediately before and after the integration began on 1 July 2015, respectively. The integration period was intended to last a single year, after which further transformation would be referred to as *reform*.

Given that neither agency was achieving excellence separately, is the reorganised DIBP better positioned for excellence as one department?

The RAND Corporation's assessment was designed to examine how the integrated organisation has been able to integrate and eliminate weaknesses and reinforce strengths across five focus areas: (1) intelligence, (2) investigations, (3) detention, (4) integrity and corruption, and (5) learning and development.

To accomplish this, RAND conducted an examination of relevant documents. Each was reviewed and catalogued, with specific attention towards findings and recommendations identified in previous studies, reports, and assessments.[2] The information in the documents was augmented through in-person and telephone interviews with the DIBP sponsors and DIBP personnel. The findings of the RAND analysis are presented in this report.

Analysis of Operational Effectiveness, 2014–2016

In examining the operational effectiveness of the newly formed department, RAND analysed data during the period of 2014–2016. This analysis focused on developing quantitatively informed trends. Two overarching themes during this period were the increased operational tempo and the ongoing reorganisation.

The study team conducted the analysis using a combination of research techniques. The study team: (1) developed an analysis and evaluation plan, (2) collected and analysed data concerning the integration, and (3) conducted an organisational analysis and drafted the final report. Throughout the study, RAND was well supported by representatives of the DIBP.

Initial study efforts focused on the evaluation of the requirements specified in the original integration directive documents, the development of an evaluation plan (in coordination with the DIBP), an analysis of the existing data concerning the integration progress to date, and an overall assessment of the performance of the DIBP. Formal deliverables were provided in accordance with the specified timelines of the request for quotation.

The RAND team's assessment was designed to examine how the integrated organisation has been performing in the areas of operational effectiveness and efficiency, building capabilities, and cultural and workforce issues.

A modified framework was employed to conduct the analysis; this framework was developed jointly between the DIBP and RAND and was based on a U.S. Government Accountability Office framework that examined the U.S. Department of Homeland

---

[2] A number of these works are classified and only available to those having an appropriate security clearance. We have noted the classified nature of these works whenever we cite or refer to them here. Any mentions we have made of these works and the information contained therein have been cleared for public release by RAND's sponsors within the DIBP.

Security's efforts towards the integration of management functions. Modifications were designed to be more operationally focused while still allowing assessment of the management functions integrated within the DIBP. The specific areas RAND assessed were (1) operational effectiveness and efficiency, (2) culture and personnel, (3) capability, (4) action plan, and (5) monitoring progress.

Study Caveats

The timing of the RAND assessment—less than a year after the integration was officially initiated—means that full annual data for 2016 were not available. Therefore, about half of the data end with 2015, providing approximately six months of operational information regarding the effects of the integration. Additionally, the data largely came from prepared reports in different formats and with different time horizons and embedded assumptions. As a result, the RAND team made a variety of assumptions during the course of the analysis to allow for longitudinal comparisons to be made.

CHAPTER TWO

The Case for Change

Overall Findings

Analysis indicates that the Customs and Immigration organisations, as well as the government of Australia, understood that systemic challenges were present, which required reform within the customs, immigration, and border-security mission space.

The need for reform was based on a number of assessments going back almost a decade. This documentation was coupled with the realisation that licit (and illicit) trade and travel were likely to increase and that budgets were likely to decline. These factors indicated that efforts in the mission space had to become more operationally effective and efficient.

Systemic shortfalls were observed in the operations of the Customs and Immigration organisations individually, indicating that reform was both necessary and inevitable. So while the integration was a vehicle for achieving change and gaining operational effectiveness, a transformation of the two organisations regardless of integration would have been required because of observed shortfalls. The integration allowed for gaining efficiencies, in addition to the professionalisation of the mission area, the workforce, and the capacities of the newly formed DIBP.

While the need for reform was well established in the official documents provided to RAND, many recommendations dating back to the earliest documents dealing with shortfalls in Immigration (such as the Comrie and Palmer reports) either had not been addressed or had been only partially addressed during the period of 2005 to 2015.[1]

Although modest changes had been implemented between 2005 and 2014 in response to emergent issues, such as the Alvarez and Rau case findings that documented these Immigration shortfalls,[2] little indication of a comprehensive transfor-

---

[1] Neil Comrie, *Inquiry into the Circumstances of the Vivian Alvarez Matter*, Canberra: Commonwealth Ombudsman, September 2005; Mick Palmer, *Inquiry into the Circumstances of the Immigration Detention of Cornelia Rau*, Canberra: Commonwealth of Australia, July 2005.

[2] Neil Comrie, *Inquiry into the Circumstances of the Vivian Alvarez Matter*, Canberra: Commonwealth Ombudsman, September 2005; Mick Palmer, *Inquiry into the Circumstances of the Immigration Detention of Cornelia Rau*, Canberra: Commonwealth of Australia, July 2005.

mation has been seen. The implemented changes were targeted to address the specific shortfalls but not necessarily the overarching issue of the professionalisation of Immigration. In a similar manner, evidence exists that Customs had taken significant steps towards reform after the establishment of a 2013 task force to implement anticorruption reforms, yet no overarching reform or professionalisation of the organisation was undertaken.

With the recommendations of the National Commission of Audit in 2013 "to merge the border control functions" of the DIBP and Customs into a "single, integrated border agency," the reform effort dramatically changed trajectory, setting the stage for integration and comprehensive reform of the customs, immigration, and border-security mission space.[3]

Several overarching conclusions concerning this reform are in order:

- The 2013 National Commission of Audit recommendation served as a catalyst and strategic guidance for Immigration and Customs reform. This recommendation built on then–Prime Minister Kevin Rudd's 2008 National Security Statement and the related *Report of the Review of Homeland and Border Security* (Smith Review), which focused on coordinating overall national security arrangements.[4]
- Neither Immigration nor Customs had the professionalisation required of a modern border-management organisation. The need for transformation of the mission space had been well documented over almost a decade.
- With implementation of the integration formally starting in July 2015, the leadership began a top-down effort to improve the operational effectiveness and efficiency of the combined Immigration and Customs organisation. Analysis supports the conclusion that, despite the turbulence of the reduced resources and increased operational tempo resulting from integration, the newly formed DIBP saw overall positive trends in performance.
- In assessing the capacity of the pre-integration organisations, interviewees consistently used common themes—such as lack of leadership, lack of role clarity, lack of process documentation, lack of cooperation, lack of professionalism—to describe their views from both inside and outside the organisations. The known corruption issues were also raised, in particular the Sydney Airport Customs corruption.
- Until the integration, Australia had never had an organisation solely for border management. This resulted in a lack of coordination within the mission space

[3] DIBP, *Department of Immigration and Border Protection: Machinery of Government Changes*, Canberra, undated; National Commission of Audit, *Towards Responsible Government: Phase One*, Canberra: Commonwealth of Australia, February 2014, pp. 207–208.

[4] Kevin Rudd, "National Security Statement," speech to the House of Representatives, Canberra, 4 December 2008. The Smith Review is described in Anthony Bergin, *A Safer Australia: Meeting the Challenges of Homeland Security*, Barton: Australian Strategic Policy Institute, 30 January 2009.

of border management. The integration and subsequent reform resulting in the newly formed DIBP should provide a more efficient and effective response to border-management issues and further assist in the deployment of resources.
- Analysis indicates that there was an absence of a solid plan for execution and a lack of written documentation for capacity-building and workforce professionalisation during the first six months of the integration. This resulted in a loss of momentum that has since been rectified.
- Evidence also supports the conclusion that there was general dissatisfaction within the workforce early in the integration. Furthermore, the capacity to ensure a professional DIBP with established goals, objectives, milestones, metrics, and foundational documents (e.g., learning, education and career paths) was not put in place. Continuing to engage the workforce will be essential to the long-term prospects for reform.
- Shortly after the implementation of the integration, the efforts stalled; in early 2016, efforts were reenergised. This included the development of foundational documents that established processes and procedures for border-management, professionalisation, and talent-management efforts.
- The one-year time frame for completing the integration was assessed to be overly ambitious by several of those interviewed. The challenges of integrating two organisations with long, proud histories of service and two very different entrenched cultures were underestimated.
- Managing workforce expectations and communicating with the workforce were two important shortfalls that were identified consistently by senior leaders interviewed as part of this effort.

Examination of Five Key Areas

Based on the documentation provided to the RAND study team, five areas were identified for further examination. The goal of the analysis was to understand the rationale for the integration through the lenses of these high-profile areas. They included (1) intelligence, (2) investigations, (3) detention, (4) integrity and corruption, and (5) learning and development.

Intelligence

This section examines the deficiencies noted in advance of the integration of the two organisations into the DIBP and the efforts made since to develop a strong intelligence function. Of note, in earlier documents (i.e., pre–July 2015), intelligence was an area identified as having many important shortfalls that required addressing.

Clear differences existed in the pre-integration area between Customs and Immigration. These disparities can be seen in a variety of measures, from the size of the intelligence functions between the organisations to the view of the role that each was attempting to carve out.

Immigration was formally a facilitative, social-policy organisation that was not allocated national security responsibilities, while Customs was a law-enforcement agency with a definite national security filter governing its operations.

The result was that, when the integration began, Customs, with its larger staff and broader vision for its role, served as the foundation for the new combined organisation. But this is not to imply that the Customs intelligence function was properly performing for achieving the goals and objectives that would be laid out as part of the integration and broader reform.

Pre-Integration Findings

Overall

Throughout the histories of Customs and Immigration, neither organisation did well in consistently sharing intelligence with each other or across the government. During the interviews, several leaders commented about the inability of the former organisations to develop intelligence, share information and intelligence, and collaborate effectively, because of a lack of a common view of the border threats. Some interviewees who had been in other government departments commented about the difficulty in communicating and coordinating with the both the Customs and Immigration organisations. Difficulties were made more profound by the lack of a centralised data-storage capacity.

Other common themes from the interviews were the lack of a professional intelligence workforce and the differences in cultures with regard to the views on intelligence. Most of the workforce had never served in intelligence elements other than in one of the two organisations. While Customs did have a modest element that performed many intelligence functions, Immigration only had a small tactical organisation, which performed compliance with the *Migration Act 1958* rather than national security intelligence. Neither organisation had the capacity to provide the full range of intelligence products.

However, intelligence shortfalls were being addressed by Customs in the pre-integration phase. Examples of efforts to modernise the intelligence functions in Customs included the following:

- Intelligence staff had grown to approximately 350–400 personnel who were distributed around the country, with the majority based in Sydney, Melbourne, and Brisbane. Most staff members were located in regional offices and worked as tactical analysts or liaison officers or performed a targeting function (e.g., cargo or passenger risk assessment—with high-risk selections referred to as the *examination areas*).
- A centralised intelligence function was also in the early stages just prior to the integration. Starting around 2011–2012, the targeting functions began to transi-

tion to a centralised model. Prior to this, each region did separate cargo-targeting. The aim was to eventually set up the National Cargo Targeting Centre in one location that did cargo-targeting for the entire country.

- These centralised functions were primarily run out of Canberra (e.g., strategic intelligence, training and development, data analytics, and executive coordination); however, there were some centralised functions run out of regions (e.g., a target-development triage function based in Brisbane).
- The majority of intelligence products were disseminated through the Integrated Intelligence Environment, a SharePoint system that the majority of Customs staff had access to. The intelligence products uploaded to the Integrated Intelligence Environment included Customs products and domestic and international law-enforcement products shared by partner agencies. The majority of intelligence products were tactical intelligence reports (predominately based on reports of detections or suspected illegal imports of drugs and firearms and money laundering).
- In Canberra, there was a dedicated team set up to work on intelligence concerning people-smuggling. This team also had access to the Department of Defence's classified systems. Additionally, there was a small cell dedicated to national security and proliferation intelligence that had access to the high-classification defence systems.
- Customs conducted a number of classified Strategic Intelligence Assessments.
- Concerning the differences in cultures between the organisations, one interviewee noted that Immigration was a facilitative, social-policy organisation and not part of the national security apparatus, while Customs was a law-enforcement agency with a definite national security filter governing its operations. These two views directly translated into differences in the way each organisation approached intelligence. As a result, Immigration had a very small staff—approximately 20 personnel. Their efforts were largely dedicated to *Migration Act 1958* noncompliance and illegal maritime arrivals (IMAs) rather than national security concerns.

Information-Sharing

The need for greater information-sharing was identified in the 2007–2010 *Australian Customs Strategic Statement* (Classified), which called for jointly leveraging customs' and other agencies' "intelligence, examination and investigation capabilities."

Furthermore, the effectiveness of the intelligence-based approach was seen in 2012, when collaborative efforts with Customs and the Australian Federal Police resulted in the seizure of illegal firearms.

In the 2013 *Australian Border Management Strategy* (Classified), a compelling case was made for better use of intelligence for information-sharing. The rationale for needing to increase information-sharing is directly related to the expected increases in "legitimate trade and travel while also protecting the border and the community from a wide range of threats." The strategy calls for "intelligence-led, risk-based" enhancements in addition to greater collaboration among government, industry, international partners, and the public.

Based on this new strategy from 2013, progress was made towards better use of information-sharing in targeting drug-trafficking and other illicit activities.

Technology for Improving Border Management

The 2013 *Australian Border Management Strategy* (Classified) called for direct infusions of technology for the intelligence-management process; risk-based focus on high-risk people, cargo, vessels, and environments; enhanced technical communications systems and fusion techniques; and advanced data analytics. The strategy addresses the need for infusion of technology to improve efforts at the border; documents and interviews indicate there is a mix of ongoing programs and aspirational effort in place. A continued need for centralised data storage existed, which neither department had prior to integration.

Another 2013 report—*Operation Heritage—A Joint Investigation of Alleged Corrupt Conduct Among Officers of the Australian Customs and Border Protection Service at Sydney International Airport (Interim Report)*—highlights the benefits of "intelligence-led interdiction," which includes the use of technology in targeting.[5] This report details the importance of technological enhancements to keep pace with the growing operational tempo and increasing sophistication of the potential violators.

Career-Mapping, Training, Learning, and Development

The broad category of the need for career paths, training, learning, and development was a discussion topic prior to the integration of the organisations. However, no specific links to the intelligence community or intelligence professionals were seen in the pre-integration phase. This would change after integration.

Findings After Integration

Overall

Major strides have been made in building a 21st-century intelligence function within the integrated DIBP. Efforts to link the intelligence function—horizontally with the government and vertically across the department—are ongoing.

Over the course of the integration period, from 1 July 2015 to 30 June 2016, an effort driven from the top down to develop an intelligence capability had been undertaken. The newly organised element has been designed to link horizontally with other government departments and agencies, as well as to hierarchically support DIBP elements managing the department, operationally engaging on issues, and conducting

---

[5] Australian Commission for Law Enforcement Integrity, *Operation Heritage—A Joint Investigation of Alleged Corrupt Conduct Among Officers of the Australian Customs and Border Protection Service at Sydney International Airport (Interim Report)*, Canberra, February 2013.

investigations. This emerging capability is also designed to support tactical issues at the border in real time and to look strategically at emerging threats that are likely to develop.

While much has been accomplished towards integration and reform, there are continuing efforts to develop the professional workforce and an intelligence function capable of supporting Australia's border-management requirements now and in the future. One interviewee stated it would likely take four years for the full effects of the reform to be put in place.

Intelligence Capability Review

The 2016 *Integrated Intelligence Capability Review* (Classified) included 107 intelligence and intelligence-related recommendations. The review proposed a significant restructuring of the Intelligence Division, to comprise five branches and be aimed at providing a strategic and central intelligence-coordination function, focused attention on thematic issues and established mission sets, an expanded tactical intelligence capability to provide real-time intelligence support, and a strategic branch to develop the department's strategic border-intelligence assessments, as well as to coordinate the Intelligence Division's activities. Given the five-year transformation plan that is ongoing, intelligence reform is under way but certainly not completed. The broad nature of the review encompasses the full range of intelligence functions, including additional calls for information-sharing and employing technology to more effectively and efficiently manage customs, immigration, and border issues. For example, the report contains significant detail about the offices and entities that must be involved in information-sharing activities.

Another example of the comprehensive nature of the reform called for in the intelligence review is the establishment of a strategic branch to develop the department's strategic border-intelligence assessments and coordinate the Intelligence Division's activities. The intelligence review also called for and defined the reorganisation of Immigration's intelligence functions and structures to manage the increasing complexity and number of interactions at the borders. Regarding the rationalising of the intelligence products, the report called for six basic formats: strategic, thematic, tactical and targeting, profiles and alerts, intelligence report, and departmental briefing note.

Technology for Improving Border Management

The intelligence review's recommendation to develop a technology road map demonstrates an important commitment to incorporating technology into future DIBP intelligence efforts and should ensure a rationalisation amongst doctrine, requirements, personnel, and technology that will likely lead to increased effectiveness and efficiency in customs, immigration, and border activities. Future investment in systems to create a single access point for intelligence data will also contribute to increased effectiveness and efficiency.

Career-Mapping, Training, Learning, and Development

With the May 2016 Learning Development Strategic Plan, efforts to develop formal career-mapping, training, learning, and education programs were set in motion.[6] A centrepiece of these efforts was standing up the ABF College on 1 July 2015, which demonstrated leadership commitment to the workforce and the reorganisation. Furthermore, the intelligence area developed procedures for career-mapping, training, learning, and education. Although the concept has been developed, the development of the full program (including the intelligence technologist profile, which describes key attributes for this position) continues to evolve. Additionally, the curriculum continues to evolve, including the assignment of mandatory training and education requirements.

Assessment

The reports leading up to the integration of Customs and Immigration into a single government department on 1 July 2015 were consistent regarding the need for intelligence reform and highlighted many symptoms that needed to be addressed.

However, Customs had recognised the need for reform in the 2011–2012 period and had started to implement changes to develop an intelligence function. These early efforts translated into an ability to target suspect shipments at the operational level.

Because Customs had developed a more robust intelligence function, when the organisations were combined, Customs served as the foundation for this new combined organisation. Interviewees also highlighted that this early effort at reform was beneficial and improved the intelligence function within Customs, but the effort did not include the broader reform envisioned during the post-integration stage.

Table 2.1 provides additional detail about the pre- and post-integration periods.

Several important reports going back as far as 2007—beginning with the 2007–2010 *Customs Strategic Statement* (Classified) and including such documents as the Australian Public Service Commission *Capability Review*,[7] *Operation Heritage* report,[8] and the Integrity Commissioner report findings and recommendations[9]—highlighted major shortfalls and identified recommendations and fixes that could or needed to be implemented. Many of these pre-integration reports indicated that change was already occurring across parts of the organisation, including in the intelligence mission space.

---

[6] DIBP, *Deputies Committee Brief: Learning and Development Strategic Plan*, Canberra, 20 May 2016.

[7] Australian Public Service Commission, *Capability Review Action Plan: Australian Customs and Border Protection Service*, Canberra, 2013.

[8] Australian Commission for Law Enforcement Integrity, *Operation Heritage—A Joint Investigation of Alleged Corrupt Conduct Among Officers of the Australian Customs and Border Protection Service at Sydney International Airport (Interim Report)*, Canberra, February 2013.

[9] Australian Commission for Law Enforcement Integrity, *Operation MYRRH—An Investigation into "Private" Illicit Drug Use by Certain Australian Customs and Border Protection Service Officers*, Canberra: Commonwealth of Australia, January 2014.

Table 2.1
Intelligence Assessment

Pre-Integration	Post-Integration
• Both organisations had – lack of consistent information-sharing – need for technology to become more effective and efficient in border-management activities – need for standardised training curricula and career paths – lack of centralised access to intelligence information – no strategic intelligence function • Customs had already started to build the capacity to support a national targeting capability focused on operational needs	• *Integrated Intelligence Capability Review* (Classified) included 107 intelligence and intelligence-related recommendations, such as – calls for information-sharing – effectively employing technology – efficiently managing customs, immigration, and border issues • Other enhancements included – development of a technology road map for intelligence – the 2016 Learning Development Strategic Plan to develop formal career-mapping, training, learning, and education programs – the systems-related investment in development of a future single intelligence data storage system – the hiring of intelligence professionals to build capacity

However, these reports also highlighted that more foundational change would be required to develop a 21st-century border-management capability.

The 2016 *Integrated Intelligence Capability Review* (Classified) continued on this path and highlighted the ongoing necessity of significant reform within the intelligence mission area. The report convincingly laid out the issues and prescribed recommendations that must be and are being undertaken.

Document reviews and interviews indicate that intelligence reform is well under way. However, given that there is a five-year transformation plan, many of these efforts are in the early stages of implementation. Additionally, several senior leaders interviewed for this study highlighted both how far the intelligence function has progressed over the past year and how far the intelligence function has to go to develop intelligence elements comparable with those in other departments.

Investigations

This section provides analysis on the topic of investigations. This section includes external investigations dealing with operational immigration and customs issues, as well as internal investigations of the workforce.

Of the documents reviewed, less than 5 percent had recommendations that specifically mentioned investigations. However, this does not mean that investigations as a topic has not been addressed adequately. Because the DIBP is a law-enforcement organisation and a large majority of the work of the organisation surrounds investigations, many of the other topic areas included or were related to investigatory work. For example, as discussed in the intelligence section above, information-sharing is directly related to investigations, although information-sharing has not been specifically called out in this manner.

Pre-Integration Findings

Prior to the integration, several areas were highlighted with respect to investigations. Most notably, not enough emphasis was placed on employing proper rules and procedures when conducting investigations. There was minimal formal training on roles and authorities and no cross-training of officers across all functions of the Immigration mission. Training focused on the tactical issues associated with investigations.

Although not directly an investigation issue, deficiencies were also noted in pre-employment screening for suitability of the workforce. In Customs, no system existed for universally vetting officers prior to 2010, when the Organisational Suitability Assessment (OSA) vetting commenced. Between 2010 and 2014, Customs processed 6,522 applications. The OSA was combined with the mandatory baseline minimum clearance level. In Immigration, the requirement for all officers to acquire a minimum of baseline security clearance through the Australian Government Security Vetting Agency (AGSVA) was not enforced.

Concerning operational investigations, in particular, the 2005 Comrie Report highlights an inquiry that recommended training programs for compliance and investigations.[10] The report specified that training for Immigration officers must include "focus on objectivity in decision making and a strong warning that false assumptions will contribute to poor decisions." The finding further highlighted that "all staff at DIMIA [the Department of Immigration and Multicultural and Indigenous Affairs] should be reminded of the need for great care in the spelling and recording of names in files and records." The implications of these findings are clear; this lack of precision in managing administrative decisions created an environment where serious mistakes could occur.

The 2013 *Border Management Strategy* (Classified) report highlighted the importance of joint investigations with Customs and the Australian Federal Police. The result was the halting of an illegal shipment of firearms. Approximately six months prior to the integration, a number of reports emphasised the need for enhanced skillsets for task management, functional law-enforcement skills, and cross-domain (such as aviation and waterfront) investigations.

Also in this 2013 time frame, an internal Immigration assessment characterised investigations teams in several state offices as "unviable."[11] The document went on to highlight that the Australian Federal Police did not have the resources to conduct criminal investigations for all Australian Public Service agencies and so these are out-

---

[10] Neil Comrie, *Inquiry into the Circumstances of the Vivian Alvarez Matter*, Canberra: Commonwealth Ombudsman, September 2005.

[11] Quoted in Jane Lee and Nick McKenzie, "Immigration Officer Warns on Risk to National Security," *Sydney Morning Herald*, 6 August 2014.

sourced to each agency. Furthermore, Immigration (at the time, the DIAC) emphasised visa cancellations over criminal investigations and focused too much on ancillary activities over core investigation business (such as the successful prosecution of high-value targets). This Immigration assessment identified four shortfalls associated with impeding investigations: high-quality executive leadership, skilled and experienced investigators, risk-based processes, and intelligence-led support. This assessment was further supported by the review of investigations undertaken by KPMG in 2013.[12] The review found that there were not adequate governance structures in place to support an effective investigation function into the future.

During interviews, the subject of a failed system-development program, which cost AUD 700 million, was identified as a wasted opportunity to reform several areas, including investigations. Had the program been successful, it would have connected several disparate systems throughout Immigration.

Findings After Integration

Many of the initiatives that Customs had started to implement regarding internal investigations served as the basis for the integrated DIBP organisation. These initiatives included statutory mandatory reporting of serious misconduct and suitability clearance for DIBP officers.

The government has taken several measures to enforce standards, ensure impartiality in investigations, and eliminate corruption. The Australian Commission for Law Enforcement Integrity (ACLEI) guides internal investigations. Its role is to "investigate law enforcement-related corruption issues, giving priority to systemic and serious corruption. ACLEI also collects intelligence about corruption in support of the Integrity Commissioner's functions . . . and [reports] annually on any patterns and trends concerning corruption in law enforcement agencies."[13] The Australian Public Service Code of Conduct was emphasised as a cornerstone of the need for public servants to be guided by value-based standards of behaviour and performance of duty.

Performance measures have also been developed, and subject-matter experts have been added to the investigation team to monitor integrity and corruption issues. Furthermore, efforts to infuse integrity into investigations included the establishment of an integrity referral officer to assist as a point of contact within the business lines. Of note, this position has since been eliminated.

Internal preemployment suitability investigations are now being incorporated into the hiring process for all DIBP staff. A backlog of integrity-checking investiga-

---

[12] DIBP, *Agenda Item 6.5: Tabling of Management Initiated Reviews (MIR); MIR Summary, Review by KPMG of Financial Audit of the Community Assistance Support (CAS) and Asylum Seeker Assistance Scheme (ASAS) Service Providers*, Canberra, 2013–2014.

[13] Queensland Organised Crime Commission of Inquiry, *Submission by the Australian Commission for Law Enforcement Integrity*, Canberra: Australian Commission for Law Enforcement Integrity, 7 July 2015, p. 2.

tions exists for many officers who have been in the department for some time but have never had such a background check.

Concerning operational investigations, several key 2016 documents provide evidence of the capacity-building that is ongoing with respect to investigations. These documents specifically provide detailed descriptions of workforce requirements (regarding vocational competency, investigations, compliance and regulation, and the border force) for dealing with investigations.[14] Another recent report that was developed after the integration addresses the need for DIBP officials to have a clear understanding of their powers and demonstrate this competency in several key areas, including investigations.[15] Finally, a May 2016 document—*Making Children Safer: The Wellbeing and Protection of Children in Immigration Detention and Regional Processing Centres* (Classified)—called out the importance of child-protection investigations.

Interviews indicated that, within the regional commands, investigations with the newly formed cross-functional teams were functioning well but perhaps not in an optimal manner. The people have been fully aligned with the expanded missions for both national security/law-enforcement and humanitarian imperatives. Although the integration of the teams has occurred, processes and procedures are continuing to be developed. Concerning investigations, one interviewee said that joint investigations are really just beginning. Indications from one interviewee are that regional commands are developing this direction in the absence of guidance from department or ABF leadership.

Progress has been made, but impediments remain. Investigations are hindered by the lack of unified platforms, including integrated information technology (IT) systems. The ongoing intelligence integration at the department level has yet to be fully pushed down to the regional commands. Building of a single department culture has been hindered by lack of progress in the learning and development area. Infrastructure—particularly related to detention activities—was cited as another issue requiring attention. All of these shortfalls have a direct effect on the ability to conduct investigations in the field.

Assessment

The 2016 *Vocational Competency Profile* provides a well-structured list of required knowledge and topics to be mastered for various levels of government officials.[16] Although this document lists an important set of skills to be taught in an ABF train-

---

[14] DIBP, *Capability and Competency Project: Project Overview*, Canberra, 2016; DIBP, *Vocational Competency Profile: Intelligence Analyst*, Canberra, 2016; DIBP, *Vocational Competency Profile: Intelligence Technologist*, Canberra, 2016; DIBP, *Vocational Competency Profile: Investigations Compliance and Regulation, Border Force*, Canberra, 2016.

[15] Assistant Secretary Australian Border Force College, *Report to Accompany BFORT Course Schedule*, Canberra: Australian Border Security, undated.

[16] DIBP, *Capability and Competency Project: Vocational Competency Profile*, Canberra, 2016.

ing curriculum, mastering and sustaining these skills over time will be a challenge for DIBP, as it is for all law-enforcement agencies.

Table 2.2 provides an overview of the findings for the pre- and post-integration periods.

Table 2.2
Investigations Assessment

Pre-Integration	Post-Integration
• Recognised shortfalls across several areas, including internal and external investigations • Lacked emphasis on proper procedures for conducting the range of investigations required of a customs, immigration, and border organisation • Recommended that training programs for compliance and investigations include the need for objectivity in decisionmaking and a strong warning that false assumptions will contribute to poor decisions	• Increased focus on how to conduct proper investigations, beginning with such fundamentals as information- and intelligence-sharing, use of technology, and decisionmaking skills • Developed the 2016 documents that specifically provide detailed descriptions of workforce requirements for dealing with investigations • Instituted major improvements to investigations that are under way based on incorporating training on related issues, such as anticorruption and workforce reporting • Implemented and developed mandatory background checks for all staff

Detention

This section examines the process of detention prior to and immediately after the integration. Two high-profile cases—those of Vivian Alvarez and Cornelia Rau—serve to define the pre-integration period and provides evidence of the need for change. Several documents leading up to the July 2015 integration continued to find shortcomings and called for fixes to the detention system. The post-integration period can be best characterised by the development of directives for implementing better policy, particularly in 2016.

Pre-Integration Findings

The Alvarez and Rau cases served as major catalysts for the internal examination of the detention system. Two high-profile 2005 government reports detailed the circumstances surrounding the Rau and Alvarez cases: the Palmer Report, which details the Rau affair,[17] and the Comrie Report, which details the Alvarez case.[18]

The Palmer Report detailing the Rau case also produced detailed findings and identified a number of key shortfalls that spanned from the actions of individual officers to departmental-level decisionmaking.

---

[17] Mick Palmer, *Inquiry into the Circumstances of the Immigration Detention of Cornelia Rau*, Canberra: Commonwealth of Australia, July 2005.

[18] Neil Comrie, *Inquiry into the Circumstances of the Vivian Alvarez Matter*, Canberra: Commonwealth Ombudsman, September 2005.

The Comrie Report provided both an exhaustive examination of the events surrounding the Alvarez case and a lengthy list of recommendations for improving the detention system. Shortfalls were noted across all areas related to detention, including investigations, use of standardised processes, decisionmaking, training, and infrastructure shortfalls (e.g., IT). This report examined in excess of 200 similar compliance, detention, and removal matters. It was a damning indictment on the organisation, and, following behind the Palmer Report, it sent a shockwave through the portfolio that lasted for many years.

For example, the report noted the need for a "compulsory checklist [to] be completed to record the actioning of a removal and that the actioning of a removal be approved by a senior compliance officer—the Officer in Charge of Compliance."[19] The interview process needed to be dynamic and designed to elicit information useful to the making of decisions about detention and removal.

The reports' findings and recommendations contained numerous areas of overlap. Both reports noted the need for better cross-agency coordination to avoid the pitfalls encountered in the two incidents. Significant policy and organisational failures were noted as well. These included leadership failures and a lack of agreed-on reporting procedures. Furthermore, training, resources, and support for officers in the field were not adequate and required too much interpretation by frontline personnel, thus allowing too much discretion and judgment on the part of junior officers.

Interviews of senior DIBP personnel also highlighted a focus on the operational requirements of managing large caseloads of irregular arrivals, rather than on fiscal discipline in the detention space prior to integration. Furthermore, the highly reactive nature of the organisation with regard to detention operations and the funding structures in place for its management was frequently noted as a shortfall.

Available documentation provides evidence that some activity to improve detention operations was occurring, but it still lacked the necessary detail to support professional detention operations. For example, in September 2007, a two-page brochure titled *The Integrated Business Model Must Do's: Transforming the Compliance, Case Management and Detention Business* provided useful information yet lacked the sort of detail called for in both the Comrie and Palmer reports.[20] It contained what can best be described as aspirational goals and objectives for Immigration business-process reform, including such topics as "single view of the client," "quality decision making," and "case management." It also provided a high-level summary of roles and responsibilities. Yet it was not, for example, the "compulsory checklist" described in the Palmer report. Of note, between the issuing of the Comrie and Palmer reports and the inte-

[19] Neil Comrie, *Inquiry into the Circumstances of the Vivian Alvarez Matter*, Canberra: Commonwealth Ombudsman, September 2005.

[20] Australian government, *The Integrated Business Model Must Do's: Transforming the Compliance, Case Management and Detention Business*, Canberra, 25 September 2007.

gration, fragmented checklists were developed and incorporated into operations. However, they were not Immigration-approved systemic checklists.

More recently, a 2011 report, the DIAC's *Strategic Plan 2011–12*, continued to highlight concerns with "administering immigration detention."[21] In 2014, an internal audit titled the *Review of Onshore Detention Facilities Maintenance and Asset Management* identified "a number of duplications, inconsistencies and inefficiencies in the management of Serco [the company hired to assist with these operations] invoices that impacted on the overall effectiveness of existing processes."[22] Taken together, indications were that many of the issues discovered in the Comrie and Palmer reports had not yet been redressed.

More broadly, the need for change across the mission space (including in detention operations and policy) was seen as a significant driver in the 2013 National Commission of Audit's recommendation "to merge the border control functions" of the DIBP and Customs into a "single, integrated border agency."[23] The commission's recommendation was based on two anticipated outcomes, the potential to generate significant savings and provide the "optimal structure" to pursue a more effective approach to border protection through "a series of integrated activities both beyond and within the border."[24]

In January 2015, a review identified major shortcomings in the area of detention operations.[25] These findings were later used to develop the *Detention Remediation Report and Corrective Action Plan* (Classified) in August 2015, shortly after the integration began.

Detention shortfalls and accompanying recommendations were also discussed in the April 2015 *Health Check of Quality Assurance Across the Department* document.[26] This internal audit considered quality-control and quality-assurance activities over four distinct areas of the department: visa application processing, removal of unlawful noncitizens, management of detention service providers, and procurement and contract management.

---

[21] DIAC, *Strategic Plan 2011–12*, Canberra, 1 July 2011.

[22] DIBP, *Review of Onshore Detention Facilities Maintenance and Asset Management,* Canberra, October 2014.

[23] DIBP, *Department of Immigration and Border Protection: Machinery of Government Changes*, Canberra, undated; National Commission of Audit, *Towards Responsible Government: Phase One*, Canberra: Commonwealth of Australia, February 2014, pp. 207–208.

[24] National Commission of Audit, *Towards Responsible Government: Phase One*, Canberra: Commonwealth of Australia, February 2014. Based on these stated goals and analysis, which identified potential for AUD 480.5 million savings over four years and the elimination of 480 full-time positions (or 3.4 percent), the efficiency measure was approved.

[25] Department of the Prime Minister and Cabinet, *Martin Place Siege: Joint Commonwealth—New South Wales Review*, State of New South Wales, January 2015.

[26] DIBP, *Health Check of Quality Assurance Across the Department*, Canberra, April 2015.

Findings After Integration

Efforts to reform the detention area are well documented in the February 2016 *Detention Remediation Report* (Classified) developed by the Detention Assurance Team that had been established. The report documents systemic changes that were incorporated into this critical immigration and national security area. The 26 February 2016 Detention Correction Plan provides an exhaustive review of the recommendations and their status in building towards a comprehensive detention system.

As part of the reorganisation, the DIBP undertook efforts to build capacity in the planning, programming, requirement-development, and budgeting functions of the department; although they are in the early stages, these efforts should improve the department's operational capacity across the DIBP mission space, including the detention area.

The process to significantly reform in the detention mission space has been led by a deputy secretary. The *Detention Remediation Report* (Classified) recommended that the department build the capabilities needed to manage the detention system into the future.

The Phase One report by the National Commission of Audit highlighted that, in the area of detention operations, progress had been made in a number of the detention metrics.[27] In particular, the number of detainees had been reduced following the integration implementation.

Additionally, a number of findings in the documents and control measures have been implemented in 2016. For example, the Serco Immigration Services Reporting Dashboards provide necessary structure for measuring detention operations. Also being implemented are a new detention placement model and better risk assessments and management of detainees.

Efforts are under way to address all aspects of the detention system. First, as part of the larger effort to professionalise the DIBP, the March 2016 *Strategy Handbook* has been developed and employed for guiding the efforts in the detention area, amongst other topic areas.[28] Second, such areas as escapees, the well-being of detainees (with a particular focus on the protection of children and families), and the mental health of detainees are being considered within the newly developed documentation.

As an example, a May 2016 document, *Making Children Safer: The Well-Being and Protection of Children in Immigration Detention and Regional Processing Centres* (Classified), notes that "since the Child Protection Panel (the Panel) commenced its work in March 2015, there has been a profound change to the immigration detention environment and . . . at the regional processing centre (RPC) in Nauru." This report

---

[27] National Commission of Audit, *Towards Responsible Government: Phase One*, Canberra: Commonwealth of Australia, February 2014.

[28] DIBP, *Strategy Handbook*, Canberra, March 2016.

put in place a capability in the immigration detention network to address potential child abuse.

Efforts are also under way to ensure that the roles and authorities of officers within the detention system are understood. This includes the leadership; the May 2016 Child Protection Panel's *Making Children Safer: The Wellbeing and Protection of Children in Immigration Detention and Regional Processing Centres* (Classified) listed such recommendations as ensuring that "Detention Superintendents and Field Compliance Operations Superintendents have the necessary authority and knowledge to fulfil their accountabilities under the Framework" have been identified and are being implemented. This increased structure and guidance will be important to building the professionalism necessary for dealing with detainees.

Interviews with senior DIBP staff indicated that a significant review of detention capability is under way. A departmental report is in the process of being finalised that will provide recommendations to further strengthen the efficiency and cost-effectiveness of detention operations, as well as recast the role of detention into a more strategic context, connected to detention priorities and focused on the detention of higher-risk persons while enabling status resolution of others in the community.

Assessment

Early reports and assessments indicated that shortfalls existed in the area of detention operations. Documented incidents from as early as 2005 with the Alvarez and Rau cases and the related investigatory reports indicated these shortfalls and made recommendations for mitigating the problems. However, reports leading up to the integration time frame indicated that, despite recognition of these issues, problems were still being uncovered in the detention mission area.

With the beginning of the integration in July 2015, the data collected to evaluate operational performance highlighted that improvements had been made in several of the detention operation areas. Metrics associated with the number of people in detention, for example, indicated a reduction in the total number of people with a detained status. Interviews with senior DIBP personnel also pointed to such metrics as reduced numbers of detention incidents in the context of an increasingly higher-risk detention population. This reflects improvement in an important aspect of professionalism that was lacking in the former organisation.

Also noteworthy is the development of documentation for managing and conducting detainee operations based on recommendations from previous reports. It is still too early to assess how well the recommendations and the reorganisation will be implemented, but initial efforts have been positive.

However, although Immigration had received repeated recommendations, commencing with the Palmer and Comrie reports in 2006, to fix systemic issues in its dealings with people at the border and in the detention network, many of the same systemic issues were identified in later reports, including the Moss Review and the

2016 Child Protection Panel's *Making Children Safer: The Wellbeing and Protection of Children in Immigration Detention and Regional Processing Centres* (Classified).[29]

Table 2.3 provides an overview of the findings for the pre- and post-integration periods.

Table 2.3
Detention Assessment

Pre-Integration	Post-Integration
• The Alvarez and Rau cases served as major catalysts for self-examination of the detention system • For example, one requirement called for the need for a "compulsory checklist [to] be completed to record the actioning of a removal and that the actioning of a removal be approved by a senior compliance officer—the Officer in Charge of Compliance"[a] • Some activity to improve detention operations was occurring, but it still lacked the necessary detail to support professional detention operations • There was a large backlog of IMA cases	• The DIBP has undertaken efforts to build capacity in the planning, programming, requirement-generation, and budgeting functions supporting detention operations • While in the early stages, these efforts should improve the department's operational capacity across the DIBP mission space, including within the detention area • Progress in developing guidance and documentation has been made and can be seen in the following: – DIBP's *Strategy Handbook*,[b] which supports the general push towards building a professional DIBP organisation – documentations on escapees and dealing with child detainees – leadership documentation to ensure that "Detention Superintendents and Field Compliance Operations Superintendents have the necessary authority and knowledge to fulfill their accountabilities under the Framework"[c]

[a] Neil Comrie, *Inquiry into the Circumstances of the Vivian Alvarez Matter*, Canberra: Commonwealth Ombudsman, September 2005, p. 33.

[b] DIBP, *Strategy Handbook*, Canberra, March 2016.

[c] Child Protection Panel, *Making Children Safer: The Wellbeing and Protection of Children in Immigration Detention and Regional Processing Centres*, 2016 (Classified).

Integrity and Corruption

This section focuses on workforce integrity and corruption issues and reforms. Corruption was an ongoing risk. However, the organisations did not sense this threat until the first cases were discovered. This became an important contributing factor that served as a stimulus for the integration. A more detailed discussion of the issue will be undertaken later in the report in the "Learning and Development" section, but its importance mandated a mention in this section as well.

Because of Immigration's service-delivery orientation, the awareness of corruption risks in that organisation was extremely low and largely limited to overseas operations. This resulted in blindness and a less-than-robust response to the risks of corruption in immigration decisionmaking.

[29] DIBP, *MIR Summary—Nauru Review by Philip Moss*, Canberra, undated.

Customs started an integrity reform process in 2010 and made progress in implementing measures to reduce the risk of corruption and infiltration by organised crime. This represented a four-year head start on the Immigration department.

Pre-Integration Findings

Interviews with senior leaders indicated the degree to which corruption and integrity issues had seized Customs. One individual noted, "Workforce corruption shook the organisation to its core and was the burning platform" that led to initial calls for reform. The 2010 reform process undertaken by Customs was important for setting the foundation for addressing corruption and integrity issues. However, despite the new emphasis on integrity and corruption, several high-profile infractions had been noted since 2010.

Several factors were attributed to the noted shortfalls. A lack of management and leadership at the border, an inability to properly allocate resources to the highest priorities, and gaps in processes and direction contributed to a climate in which corruption and integrity shortfalls were allowed to develop. Failure to consistently vet individuals—both initially and during the course of their service—created a culture with a lack of accountability across the workforce, from senior leaders to individual Customs and Immigration officers. Many officers did not have security clearances. Additionally, universal standards for vetting officers and providing clearances in line with Commonwealth standards were not developed until after 2010.

Prior to 2010, Customs undertook its own security clearances in house and had developed and implemented a requirement that all individuals (employees, contractors, seconded staff and so on) who required nonpublic access to Customs assets required a minimum of a Protected (now known as baseline) security clearance. In addition to the security clearance, Customs undertook additional checks known as "fit and proper person" checks, which examined a range of Customs-specific risk factors, such as criminal associations, compliance with border-related laws, and illicit drug usage. These checks became a step in the recruitment process for new staff. The implementation of the mandatory and universal screening within Customs commenced in the 1990s. Because of the passage of time, it is not possible to obtain specific numbers of individuals cleared during this period; however, based on available data, it appears that approximately 30,000 individuals underwent a security clearance and "fit and proper person" check prior to 2010.

In October 2010, security clearance processing was centralised in the AGSVA. At this time, the requirement for all individuals to obtain a minimum baseline clearance was continued, albeit via the AGSVA, with the additional "fit and proper person" checks continuing to be undertaken by Customs. At the time, these checks were formally established into a discrete framework known as the OSA. Both the minimum baseline security clearance and the OSA continued to be applied universally to all individuals who required nonpublic access to Customs assets. Customs finalised 9,232 OSA assessments.

The DIAC Strategic Plans (2010–2011 and 2011–2012) that were reviewed consistently highlighted the importance of integrity.[30] Specifically, the documents made the case for having a values-based organisation built on trust. For example, the 2011–2012 document calls for a workforce where "integrity and honesty fosters teamwork, supporting high performance throughout the department." Also called out as an important element is integrity in decisionmaking.

Prior to October 2010, Immigration conducted its own security clearance and preemployment screening checks. Security clearances were only conducted for positions that were Designated Security Assigned Positions (DSAPs) or Positions of Trust (POTs). This was in line with the *Protective Security Manual* (PSM), which was preceded by the *Protective Security Policy Framework* (PSPF).[31]

However, in October 2010, similar to Customs, Immigration's security clearance processing function was centralised in the AGSVA. Immigration retained the preemployment screening function; minimum standards for preemployment screening were met by undertaking the National Police History Check (via Crimtrac) and 100-point identification checks.

Security clearances continued to only be conducted for positions that were DSAPs or POTs, in accordance with the PSPF. These requirements are now listed under Mandatory Requirements for personnel security (PERSEC): PERSEC 3 and PERSEC 4.

In all cases where an individual required access to security classified information or systems, the department enforced this requirement consistently with its obligations under the PSPF and its predecessor, the PSM. It is therefore not appropriate for the report to characterise the security clearance requirements as not being enforced—under the PSPF, only individuals who require access to security classified material must obtain the relevant security clearance, and this requirement was adhered to by Immigration at all times.

The ACBPS's *Capability Review Action Plan* in June 2013 also highlighted the broad need for leadership and workforce reform.[32] Specific areas included "leadership behaviours, responsibilities and accountabilities through personal charters."

---

[30] DIAC, *The DIAC Strategic Plan 2010–11: A Strategic Plan to Build Stronger Migration and Visa Services*, Canberra, 2010; DIAC, *Strategic Plan 2011–12*, Canberra, 1 July 2011.

[31] See Australian Public Service Commission, "Security," in *Foundations of Government*, Canberra, 23 May 2012.

[32] Australian Public Service Commission, *Capability Review Action Plan: Australian Customs and Border Protection Service*, Canberra, 2013.

The 2013 Australian Federal Police, ACLEI, and Customs Operation Heritage conducted an in-depth investigation of corruption at the Sydney Airport.[33] The investigation included efforts to detect potential corruption in the future. One of the prescient findings in the interim report was the "inadequate preparation for the change in risk." In particular, this emerging threat was said to come from the increased threat of corrupt compromise and infiltration by organised-crime groups.

Despite recognition of the importance of integrity in the mission space, a major breach was discovered, and the report—*Operation Heritage Final Report*—was published in February 2014.[34] In the incident, eight Customs officers faced criminal charges arising from Operation Heritage, including three officers who faced charges relating to intentional inaccuracy in their evidence to the Integrity Commissioner. The conduct of five additional Customs officers—who were not charged with criminal offences—was also investigated, and appropriate disciplinary action was taken by Customs. An important realisation, according to the report, was the "strong link between integrity and organisational capability." The investigation also highlighted possible corruption issues involving Customs officers.

One result of the *Operation Heritage* report was the enactment of legislation. Specifically, the Law Enforcement Integrity Legislation Amendment Act 2012 (the LEILA Act) introduced specific anticorruption measures for Customs—such as drug and alcohol testing, the power to declare that a dismissal was for reason of serious misconduct (which modifies appeal rights), and an authority to issue binding orders relating to conduct and integrity (such as mandatory reporting of misconduct).

Another breach in workforce integrity and corruption was reported in Operation Myrrh, an investigation into illicit drug use by certain Customs officers.[35] The investigation uncovered information about three officers that indicated their involvement in a loose network of so-called social cocaine users. The officers have since resigned from the department.

The *Customs Reform Board: First Report* also highlighted integrity as an issue and made a number of important recommendations, including the "appointment of a Spe-

---

[33] Australian Commission for Law Enforcement Integrity, *Operation Heritage—A Joint Investigation of Alleged Corrupt Conduct Among Officers of the Australian Customs and Border Protection Service at Sydney International Airport (Interim Report)*, Canberra, February 2013.

[34] Australian Commission for Law Enforcement Integrity, *Operation Heritage (Final Report)—A Joint Investigation of Alleged Corrupt Conduct Among Officers of the Australian Customs and Border Protection Service at Sydney International Airport*, Canberra, February 2014.

[35] Australian Commission for Law Enforcement Integrity, *Operation MYRRH—An Investigation into "Private" Illicit Drug Use by Certain Australian Customs and Border Protection Service Officers*, Canberra: Commonwealth of Australia, January 2014.

cial Integrity Advisor to provide the Chief Executive Officer independent advice on anti-corruption measures and assurance systems."[36]

In June 2015, just prior to the integration of the DIBP, the secretary released a document with integrity measures. It states,

> Our work and the information we hold is valuable to organised crime syndicates, who actively try to circumvent border controls, reduce border integrity and threaten national security[,] and our border management activities are a significant target for criminal groups who have strong financial and other motives to infiltrate border protection agencies across the globe. Our integrity must be of the highest order and our behaviour consistent with the laws we enforce.[37]

A complementary document that came out at the same time was the secretary's professional standards message. It states,

> To perform effectively in this environment, it is critical that the Department secures and maintains the confidence of government, industry, the law enforcement community (both domestic and international) and the wider community. Central to this goal are the professionalism and integrity of staff, contractors, consultants and secondees and the ability of the Department, at an organisational level, to prevent and counter internal corruption and misconduct.[38]

To summarise the pre-integration period, corruption issues discovered in the Australian Customs Service in 2010 stimulated a reform process focussed on integrity and corruption. Mechanisms implemented from late 2010 onwards included a drug- and alcohol-management program, integrity testing, OSAs (now called Employment Suitability Clearance), mandatory reporting, outside employment declaration, declarable circumstances, and conflicts of interest.

By late 2013, the mechanisms in Customs were being implemented. At the time of the integration announcement, the Customs service had been implementing integrity measures for some three to four years. Although these efforts placed some focus on the issue, developing a culture of integrity and anticorruption was seen as requiring a systemic approach to building the foundations that would be necessary.

Findings After Integration

In the pre-integration phase, integrity and corruption issues were plaguing both organisations. Although some reforms were put in place prior to integration, in the post-integration phase and carrying through into the more comprehensive reform period, a

---

[36] Australian government, *Customs Reform Board, First Report*, Canberra: Commonwealth of Australia, June 2013.

[37] DIBP, *Integrity Measures*, Canberra, 29 June 2015, p. 1.

[38] DIBP, *Professional Standards*, Canberra, 29 June 2015, p. 1.

systemic approach was required to address the root causes of the issues. These efforts are under way.

The result was that several of the shortfalls noted above were addressed, including a lack of management at the border and an inability to develop resource trade-offs; in addition, gaps in processes and direction contributed to a climate in which corruption and integrity shortfalls were allowed to develop. Comprehensive reform efforts are under way to address leadership and management failures in the field. Doctrine, regulations, and guidance are being developed to assist in guiding how the officers perform. Professionalisation activities are being incorporated into all aspects of the DIBP officers' learning and development.

The early efforts undertaken by Customs served as a foundation for developing a culture of integrity and anticorruption in the newly formed DIBP. However, the efforts were not the type of comprehensive reform that is envisioned as part of the integration and subsequent reform process that is currently occurring.

Simultaneously with the integration in July 2015, the department released the *Building One Organisation* document as part of the Portfolio Change Management Strategy and Values and Behaviours initiative.[39] Integrity and anticorruption language was featured prominently in the document.

With regard to vetting and security clearances, a newly developed integrity framework provided guidance.[40] It established a mandatory requirement for all individuals who required nonpublic access to departmental assets (regardless of whether these were formerly owned or operated by Customs or Immigration) to have a minimum baseline security clearance and to undergo employment-suitability screening. The new employment-suitability screening process applied to the newly integrated department was known as the Employment Suitability Clearance and was based largely on the OSA framework which had operated within the former Customs organisation.

In the lead-up to integration, all existing Immigration officers who did not hold security clearances were identified and required to undergo a baseline security clearance. This work was largely completed by the integration—by then, the overwhelming majority of employees either held a security clearance or had a clearance in process with the AGSVA.

In an effort to build on the enhanced integrity efforts, several important recommendations are being incorporated as part of the integration-reform professionalisation:

- Implement better record and case management of sensitive matters by utilising Custom's upgraded IT system capability.
- Implement a collection-management strategy in association with the Intelligence Division.

---

[39] Australian government, *Building One Organisation—Pulse Check Findings Summary*, Canberra, July 2015.

[40] DIBP, *Employment Suitability and Security Screening*, Canberra, 29 June 2015.

- Implement internal mechanisms and standard operating procedures with the Integrity Assessment Committee to monitor task force referrals (case management) for DIBP tracking purposes.
- Implement stricter internal intelligence-reporting deadlines.

Additionally, a May 2016 document titled *Leadership Framework* provided a guide for DIBP leadership at all levels (see Figures 2.1 and 2.2).[41] The framework focuses on building values and holding people accountable across all grades and skill levels.

One assessment provided by a senior individual involved with developing and rolling out the integrity initiatives indicated that the framework was still being introduced to the workforce. Some immediate effects have resulted from breath-alcohol and drug testing and discussions of accountability. This same individual highlighted that

Figure 2.1
Learning and Development: Live and Promote Our Values and Behaviours

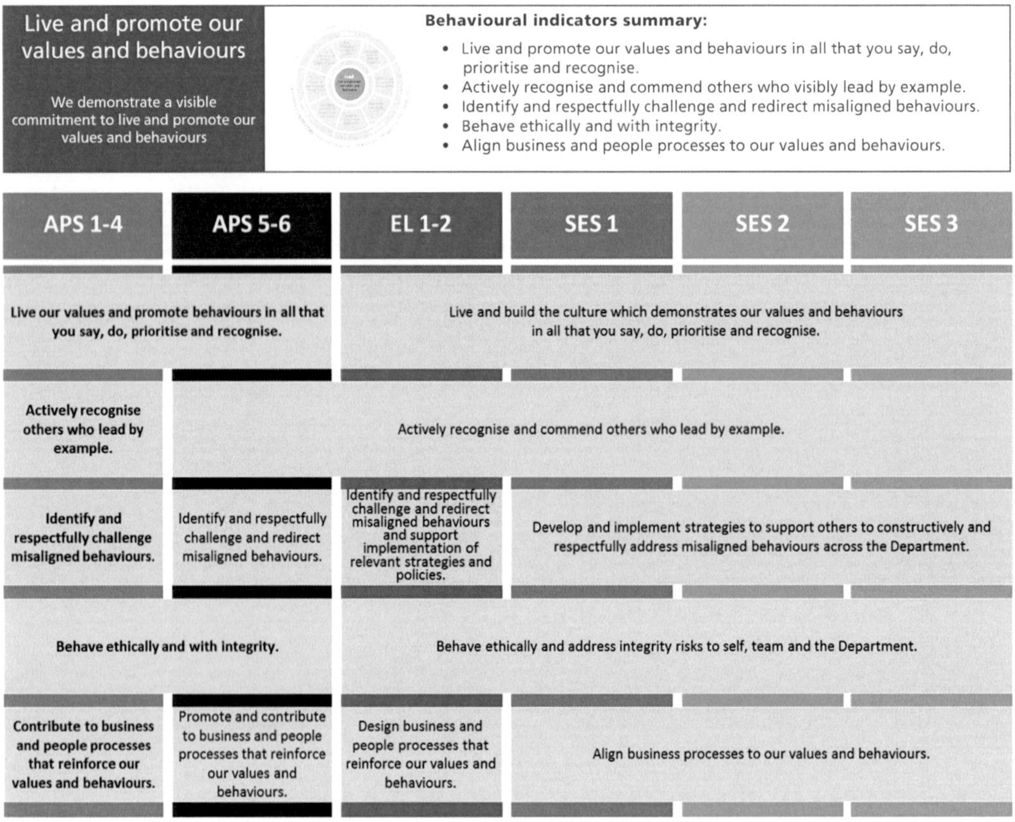

SOURCE: DIBP, *Leadership Framework*, Canberra, May 2016.
RAND *RR1713-2.1*

---

[41] DIBP, *Leadership Framework*, Canberra, May 2016.

Figure 2.2
Learning and Development: Hold Self and Each Other to Account

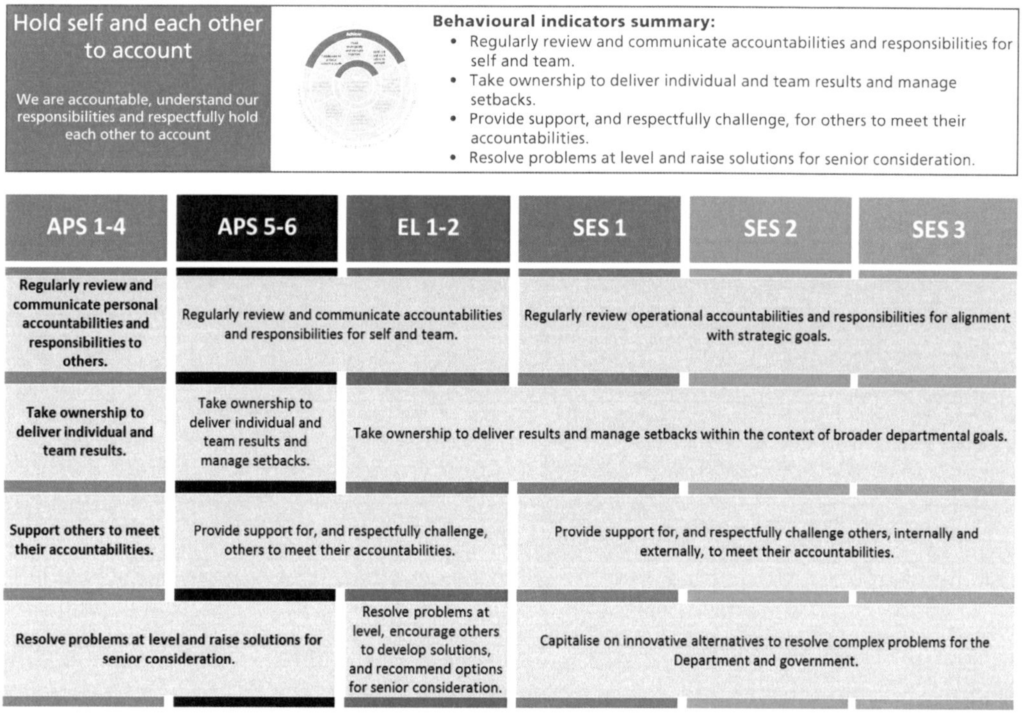

SOURCE: DIBP, *Leadership Framework*, Canberra, May 2016.
RAND *RR1713-2.2*

there is still a ways to go with screening for suitability, indicating that, at the current pace, it will take "eight years to achieve screening." Additional resources have been requested, and there remain more than 100 referred ACLEI corruption case investigations. Finally, efforts are ongoing to employ a risk-based approach to corruption, focussing on the most likely and most dangerous areas.

In addition to the DIBP *Leadership Framework*, the leader-development road map was established in May 2016. One element of this road map is highlighting the various points in an officer's career where integrity training and development will be addressed.

Failure to vet individuals—both initially and during the course of their service—had created a culture with a lack of accountability. To address these deficiencies, several areas of focus for the screening of the workforce have been established, including looking for people with links to organised crime; identifying networks within the workforce; establishing the integrity referral officer at levels accessible to the workforce; incorporating training on related topics, such as ethical decisionmaking; and continually emphasising integrity issues.

Assessment

The issue of integrity in the workforce was first seen in the documents that the RAND team reviewed in the 2010 time frame and has held a prominent place in the dialogue until the present day.

Several major breaches prior to the integration demonstrated the rationale for concerns about effectiveness and efficiency, and there was also the issue of gaining public confidence. Although early documents contained recommendations for addressing integrity and corruption, the more-recent documents have included *plans* for doing so. The degree to which these overview plans can be turned into detailed lesson plans and taught as part of the curriculum will determine how well integrity and anticorruption programs and messages can be turned into practice. Furthermore, the plans reflect programs designed to engage the total workforce, from senior leaders to junior members of the DIBP. Once these programs have been incorporated into the training and education program, their effectiveness can be better assessed.

In particular, Customs had received recommendations after the investigation of corruption allegations through the Operation Heritage and Myrrh reports. Although a reform programme to address the integrity issues began in 2013, they will continue and be challenging, even in the integrated organisation.

Despite greatly increased focus on integrity and anticorruption, individual lapses continue to occur and a backlog of internal investigations persists; building a DIBP-wide culture of integrity and anticorruption will require time and a significant expenditure of capital from senior leaders' emphasis on integrating the topics into all aspects of DIBP officers' lifecycles.

Despite the periodic lapses, there is a noteworthy finding: Whereas the lapses were previously brought to light upon being discovered by external actors, the most recent lapses have been uncovered internally, indicating greater oversight and transparency into workforce actions.

Interviews with senior personnel suggested that the workforce had begun to embrace, or at a minimum accept, the integrity and anticorruption measures that have been put in place. Such measures as drug and alcohol testing, preemployment suitability checks, and incorporating integrity and corruption training and development into the curriculum are evolving from exceptional events to normal requirements for a DIBP officer.

Table 2.4 provides an overview of the findings for the pre- and post-integration periods.

Learning and Development

This section examines the learning and development issues associated with the DIBP mission space and within the organisation, both prior to and after the integration. Many of the training, learning, and developmental shortfalls observed in the documents as early as 2005, with the Alvarez and Rau cases, were still observed as late as

Table 2.4
Integrity and Corruption Assessment

Pre-Integration	Post-Integration
• The integrity issue was first seen in the documents that the RAND team reviewed in the 2010 time frame and has held a prominent place in the dialogue until the present day • Strategic plans that were reviewed (for 2010–2011 and 2011–2012) consistently highlighted the importance of integrity • The Customs capability review in June 2013 also highlighted the broad need for leadership and workforce reform; specific topics included "leadership behaviours, responsibilities and accountabilities through personal charters"[a] • Despite growing recognition of the importance of integrity, a major breach was discovered, and the report—the Operational Heritage final report—was published in February 2014[b]	• The DIBP released the *Building One Organisation* document as part of the Portfolio Change Management Strategy and the Values and Behaviours initiative[c] • The DIBP Integrity Framework inclusion for employment suitability screening and security screening is being implemented • The department's newly developed drug and alcohol policy in May 2015 has been implemented • A leader-development road map was developed in May 2016 • Online ethics and conduct training was developed • Integrity conversations were incorporated into workforce education

[a] Australian Public Service Commission, *Capability Review Action Plan: Australian Customs and Border Protection Service*, Canberra, 2013.

[b] Australian Commission for Law Enforcement Integrity, *Operation Heritage (Final Report)—A Joint Investigation of Alleged Corrupt Conduct Among Officers of the Australian Customs and Border Protection Service at Sydney International Airport*, Canberra, February 2014.

[c] Australian government, *Building One Organisation—Pulse Check Findings Summary*, Canberra, July 2015.

immediately prior to the integration. Since the reorganisation, efforts to establish a more comprehensive approach to the workforce and organisational professionalisation have been put in place.

Pre-Integration Findings

Early pre-integration documents emphasised the need to enhance training, learning, and development to address operational shortfalls and missteps that had occurred within the customs, immigration, and border-management area. For example, a 2005 document detailing and making recommendations regarding the Alvarez case identified the need for a training program for compliance and investigation officers.[42] Although documentation indicated that some change was incorporated, evidence of broad systemic change was not observed until the reform efforts were about to begin.

Research indicated that awareness of corruption risks was extremely low and largely limited to overseas operations. This resulted in blindness to and a less-than-robust response to the risks of corruption in Immigration decisionmaking. Additionally, other efforts to increase training and officer proficiency included developing the

[42] Neil Comrie, *Inquiry into the Circumstances of the Vivian Alvarez Matter*, Canberra: Commonwealth Ombudsman, September 2005.

Immigration College for several years and attempting to improve the pace and quality of training for Immigration officers.

Throughout the pre-integration period, shortfalls in training were identified across numerous operational areas. IT training shortfalls were seen as a hindrance to information- and intelligence-sharing and operational effectiveness. Improper training contributed to loss and the improper handling of data. In several cases, officers were not able to operate basic equipment, such as close-circuit television. Lack of privacy training contributed to several incidents; as a result, recommendations from several documents highlighted the need for privacy training. Several documents highlighted shortfalls in leadership training and development, causing both operational and workforce issues.

Other important development shortfalls were in areas previously discussed, such as integrity and anticorruption and general professionalisation. Of note, the two organisations had very different cultures, which could complicate the integration process.

A July 2014 document, *The Learning and Development Strategic Plan*, highlighted the need for reform and identified several areas that must be transformed.[43] Particularly noteworthy is that this document highlighted the then-upcoming July 2015 integration as a key inflection point in changes on the horizon.

The December 2014 *Learning and Development* document captured the lack of a comprehensive program for the initial training of the border-management workforce, as well as the lack of continuing or refresher training.[44] Additionally, there was no formal cross-training in other functional areas that officers were supposed to be proficient in during their careers. Further, the document highlighted that some specialties had little or no formal training. The document stated, "The ACBPS recruit training programme has been delivered in various forms for a number of years, however had most recently been limited to training officers to work in the air traveller environment only."

Clearly, deficiencies in training, learning, and development were well understood. As late as April to June 2015, shortfalls were noted in several Senate-estimate transcripts (Classified). The need for reform was seen to extend to the earliest days of an officer's introduction into the department. Calls for a workforce transformation package included the Border Force Officer Recruit Training (BFORT). Another recurring perceived need was for training on anticorruption measures.

In fact, some actions were being undertaken to remediate these shortfalls. For example, the *Capability Review Action Plan Progress Report Fourth Quarter Report to the Australian Public Service Commission May 2014–July 2014* (Classified) discussed efforts to incorporate a "leadership framework" and new strategies for training and development.

---

[43] DIBP, *The Learning and Development Strategic Plan*, Canberra, July 2014.

[44] Australian government, *Learning and Development, ABF Recruit Training*, Canberra, December 2014.

Another preimplementation document, a vocational bulletin, was further designed to increase the professionalism of the workforce by describing training, core capabilities, duties, oaths, and additional information about how their jobs are structured.[45] This bulletin was released in March 2015 but is part of the execution planning of the reorganisation.

The discussion about vocational-training pathways was mentioned in several of the pre-integration documents, from visas to detention. Actions taken in the field contributed to observed operational shortfalls, questionable decisions, high-profile missteps, and loss of public confidence. The roots of this change can be seen in several of the documents that highlighted shortfalls in training and education, as well as decisionmaking skills.

Also highlighted were requirements for different types of training, learning, and development. For example, the visa vocational-training road map emphasised the need for the inclusion of experiential and interactive training to augment traditional classroom learning.[46]

Findings After Integration

In the pre-integration period, the planning for the ABF College was conducted. This allowed for the rapid establishment of the college immediately upon the initiation of the integration. Many of the validated and perceived shortfalls that had been identified were addressed as part of the curriculum. The college was intended to provide "dimensions of competency for Graduates to include not just task management skills, but functional law enforcement skills that can be used across many domain environments (aviation, waterfront and investigations)."[47] Such a curriculum provides the foundations for developing a professional workforce, as well as professionalisation of the reformed DIBP organisation.

Also included in this pre-integration planning was the need to augment formal classroom training. The term *blended training* was intended to complement formal classroom training, experimental learning, and targeted mentoring obtained on the job. In this regard, several initiatives from the vocational bulletin were implemented in September 2015, including the development of vocational pathways for visa processing that brought many of these different workforce developmental activities into the training, learning, and developmental process.

Several more-recent documents have served to amplify the earlier planning documents. For example, in March 2016, ABF published the *Learning Governance Model,*

---

[45] Australian Customs and Border Protection, *Australian Border Force Bulletin #3*, Canberra, March 2015.

[46] DIBP, *Visa Decision Maker Vocational Training Pathway Training Needs Analysis*, Canberra: Commonwealth of Australia, 2015.

[47] Australian government, *Learning and Development, ABF Recruit Training*, Canberra, December 2014, p. 1.

which provided guidance on selected vocational fields.[48] Later, the *Learning and Development Strategic Plan* and the high-level roadmap from May 2016 both reinforced the earlier planning documents and added additional details on workforce training.[49]

Also notable, the documents indicated that, in the post-integration period, greater attention was paid to the management of the training, learning, and developmental process. The establishment of the ABF College was an important part of this increased move towards personal professionalisation. New courses were developed. The courses transitioned from being highly focused on specialty areas to including greater emphasis on general law-enforcement issues, individual development and professionalisation, and broader roles and responsibilities. This was also seen in the interviews that were conducted; for example, several noted that integrity and anticorruption initiatives became part of the learning and development process. Other examples are the inclusion of decisionmaking skills, which had been a perceived shortfall in the pre-integration period, and the training involved in teaching officers their basic powers.

Many of the issues regarding the complexities of merging the two cultures remain today, but some ground has been gained. Interviewees suggested that efforts to develop a DIBP culture remain a work in progress. Developing common standards and cross-functional teams and using learning and development opportunities to talk about broader issues, such as leadership, accountability, integrity, and corruption, are resonating with many members of the workforce.

Regarding organisational development, a general concern identified throughout several of the interviews is about the emergence of the layering and deconfliction of functions. The concern entailed identifying the roles and responsibilities for operational, support, and departmental-level personnel. One interviewee noted, and others echoed, that, in the absence of this delineation, "operations people were doing support, support people were doing operations, and operations and support people were doing departmental functions."

One shortfall consistently noted in the interviews was a perceived lack of continued engagement by DIBP leadership. Several interviewees mentioned that the early road shows used to talk about the integration of the workforce had stopped and had not been replaced with any other engagement efforts. This was mentioned as a shortfall from all levels, from DIBP headquarters to the regional commands.

Another important set of initiatives concerned the greater emphasis on leadership as a key skill for the workforce. This topic was incorporated into curriculum within the ABF courses, as well as in stand-alone courses dedicated to leader development.

---

[48] Australian Border Force, *L&D and ABF College Board SUBMISSION—Learning Governance Model*, Canberra: Department of Immigration and Border Protection, 17 March 2016.

[49] DIBP, *The Learning and Development Strategic Plan*, Canberra, July 2014; DIBP, *Deputies Committee Brief: Learning and Development Strategic Plan*, Canberra, 20 May 2016.

A May 2016 briefing provided at a deputy commissioner's meeting indicates that some of the activities outlined in the *Learning and Development Strategic Plan* are well under way.[50] The work to mature the learning capability across the department is being funded through the learning and development and the ABF College reform work package. Both the visibility this topic is getting and the ongoing efforts bode well for long-term success. However, it remains too early to assess whether these programmes will ultimately be successful.

Establishment of a board to monitor this area provides an important organisational structure with responsibility for learning and development across the DIBP. The Learning and Development and ABF College Board is responsible for providing the overall direction on learning and development priorities across the department. The board will meet at least every three months and is accountable for ensuring that learning and development services meet the portfolio's strategic priorities, build people capability, and support cultural change.

Another important development was the establishment of the *L&D Quality Assurance Procedural Instruction* in April 2016, which outlines the department's quality-assurance process for providing consistent and quality learning and development services.[51] Quality assurance helps to continuously improve learning and development capability and maturity and to identify issues and trends that might point to systemic failures or gaps in systems, policies, or procedures. Several other important organisational adaptations have been incorporated for ensuring that these programmes receive the required emphasis.

Assessment

The history going back to the earliest documents, from 2005, indicates understanding of the need for transforming the training, learning, and development of the workforce and the organisations of the customs, immigration, and border-management entities. These early documents indicate that fixes had been incorporated. However, despite the correct diagnosis of the issues and programmes established to redress these shortfalls, they continued to be a source of concern.

Many changes have been incorporated into the training, learning, and developmental programmes of the newly formed DIBP. The extent to which these programmes will be successful and lead to greater operational effectiveness and efficiency has yet to be seen. Many of these efforts are in the early stages of implementation; therefore, the full impact cannot yet be assessed.

Concerted leadership engagement will be necessary to achieve intended outcomes. The development of a road map for managing these efforts is a positive step. Maintain-

---

[50] DIBP, *Deputies Committee Brief: Learning and Development Strategic Plan*, Canberra, 20 May 2016.

[51] DIBP, *L&D Quality Assurance Procedural Instruction*, Canberra, 7 April 2016.

ing momentum will require constant monitoring and the establishment of key metrics for monitoring progress.

Table 2.5 provides an overview of the findings for the pre- and post-integration periods.

Conclusions

Written documents and the interviews clearly demonstrated the need for change within Australia's border management. The five areas examined—(1) intelligence, (2) investigations, (3) detention, (4) integrity and corruption, and (5) learning and development—provided ample evidence of shortfalls and issues to be addressed.

The pre-integration period can be characterised by high-profile issues and organisations that demonstrated a lack of professionalism and an inability to handle the anticipated increased workflow at the border. Major shortfalls could be seen across virtually all of the systems that RAND examined.

Table 2.5
Learning and Development Assessment

Pre-Integration	Post-Integration
• Shortfalls had been observed throughout the documents, beginning with the earliest findings dealing with the Alvarez and Rau cases • Numerous recommendations and fixes had been identified • There is little evidence that the pre-integration efforts in training, learning, and development were fully incorporated—issues continued to be observed, and there were repeated calls for professionalisation of the workforce and the customs, immigration, and border-management organisations • Documents from 2014 and 2015, including *The Learning and Development Strategic Plan*,[a] were incorporated into the post-integration efforts that began in July 2015	• Many changes have been incorporated into the new training, learning, and developmental programmes of the newly formed DIBP • The extent to which these programmes will be successful and lead to greater operational effectiveness and efficiency has yet to be seen; many of these efforts are in the early stages of implementation and therefore the full impact cannot yet be assessed • Efforts have been expanded in this area to be more comprehensive and updated with a variety of topics and incorporating a variety of training, learning, and developmental techniques • Several institutions highlighted important changes that aim to distinguish these efforts from other pre-integration efforts, such as establishing – the ABF College – the Learning and Development and ABF College Board – the *L&D Quality Assurance Procedural Instruction*[b] – Learning and Development and ABF College reform work

[a] DIBP, *The Learning and Development Strategic Plan*, Canberra, July 2014.

[b] DIBP, *L&D Quality Assurance Procedural Instruction*, Canberra, 7 April 2016.

The post-integration period can best be characterised as focused activity to build the organisational capacity and professional workforce for a modern 21st-century border-management organisation. Although changes that have been incorporated into the department since the 1 July 2015 integration are impressive, continued emphasis by leadership will be needed to realise the goals and objectives of the integration and, more broadly, the more comprehensive reform that is envisioned.

The loss of momentum in the early months after the integration began (and the resulting reinvigoration of the effort several months later) should serve as a warning of the potential for the effort to stall if leadership engagement does not continue.

CHAPTER THREE

Assessing Operational Effectiveness as a Result of the Integration

Overall Findings

The DIBP has supported the government of Australia in the customs, immigration, and border-protection mission area during the period of 2014–2016, with no observable decrease in capability, while undergoing a significant reorganisation and a decrease in top-line funding. RAND examined a total of 130 operational programme performance measures. The results indicate that 64 (49 percent) met targets or were improving, 29 (22 percent) remained constant, 15 (12 percent) did not meet targets or were declining, and 22 (17 percent) were not determined (i.e., the data were either not available or the trends were not identifiable).

Overall conclusions of the analysis are presented in Table 3.1.

Despite the ongoing reorganisation and operational pace, the department has been undergoing a significant reduction in funding. The 2016–2017 budget-submission documents showed an overall departmental-level reduction in top-line funding from AUD 7.2 billion in 2015–2016 to AUD 6.8 billion in 2016–2017 (projected). The reductions out to 2019 are even more pronounced.

Analysis indicates an increasing number of legal visitors despite the decrease in departmental-level funding. For sea and air cargo, the ABF has met goals for the number of targeted inspections, which went up by 33 percent for 2014–2015 and is on track to repeat for 2015–2016. Increases in legitimate trade and travel have resulted in increased revenue from AUD 15.7 billion in 2014–2015 to AUD 18.6 billion in 2015–2016 in (projected).

Over this period, the DIBP has been involved in a significant integration of Customs and Immigration into a single department. The reorganisation was based on a well-developed 2014 plan for integration with an execution date of 1 July 2015. Departmental objectives linked to national objectives were clearly specified and formed the basis for reorganisation. The desired outcomes were established along with the functional requirements for affected organisations. One important shortfall noted pertained to the lack of identified metrics that could have supported the tracking of the reorganisation implementation.

Table 3.1
Operational Effectiveness Assessment

Category	Description	Assessment
Operational effectiveness and efficiency	Support for the customs, immigration, and border mission (i.e., operational tempo)	• No observed loss in effectiveness across operational missions • Increases in trade and travel were noted during the period • Given reductions in the budget, there has been an increase in efficiency: More than 70 percent of the operational metrics show improvement or have remained constant
Culture and personnel	Indicators of the effects on the culture of the DIBP and personnel programs	• Strong indications of support for the workforce and attempts to build a common DIBP culture • Strong leadership commitment, yet recent employee survey showed negative views concerning several key metrics, including perceptions of senior leadership • Unforeseen challenges identified in interviews regarding combining two entrenched organisations, including disparities in pay and conditions
Capability	Programs and process designed to build organisational capacity	• Little direct quantitative evidence of capability-building, yet important qualitative evidence (e.g., common human resources and financial systems, ABF College development) • Large, ongoing investments in key areas, such as intelligence, investigations, and integrity and corruption
Action plan for reorganisation	Examination of the reorganisation planning for pre- and post-execution	• Strong pre-execution plan developed, but shortfalls noted in post-integration period (i.e., did not contain adequate metrics that were defined and measurable and also included assumptions and thresholds)
Monitoring progress of reorganisation	Capabilities for monitoring the progress of the reorganisation	• Shortfalls noted in the monitoring of the integration (e.g., leadership visibility of execution progress, inadequate metrics to track progress [at both the strategic and operational levels], desire for greater communication with workforce)

In the early stages of the integration, many important programs were initiated that provided necessary momentum towards full implementation. However, evidence exists that shortly after initiation of the integration, implementation was not being adequately tracked, and the pace of execution slowed. These shortfalls were identified by the DIBP, and the result has been the establishment of the Strategic Reform Group. Particularly noteworthy, this group is under the direction of the deputy secretary, which stands in contrast to the predecessor organisation that was aligned under the first assistant secretary. This realignment will also likely improve leadership visibility for reorganisation efforts. The new organisation also has an implementation role, rather than just a monitoring and reporting role as the previous organisation had.

The internal review also identified the need to develop and track metrics across key program areas. An external contractor was enlisted to develop these metrics. While not yet being utilised, these measures could provide an important foundation for tracking departmental performance for operational effectiveness and efficiency, as well as towards fulfilling the goals of the integration. However, a noted shortfall is the nearly exclusive focus on operational metrics at the expense of strategic and reorganisation metrics and the omission of some key DIBP mission elements, such as cybersecurity and interagency collaboration (including information-sharing).

Specific Findings

Utilising the modified framework employed by the U.S. Government Accountability Office (GAO) to examine the U.S. Department of Homeland Security (DHS), RAND developed specific findings in each of the five areas listed in Table 3.1.[1] The elements of the framework have been divided into two categories, those directly related to operational elements and those related to the implementation of the integration.

Operational Elements

Operational Effectiveness and Efficiency

Progress has been made in increasing overall effectiveness and efficiency within the customs, immigration, and border-patrol mission space. The combination of Customs and Immigration is projected to result in savings in dollars and personnel through 2020. The savings in the top line have begun, while the personnel savings are expected later in the reorganisation. Additionally, the DIBP-provided performance metrics were analysed to assess the department's operational trends. A total of 130 programme performance measures were examined. The results indicate that 64 (49 percent) met targets or were improving, 29 (22 percent) remained constant; 15 (12 percent) did not meet targets or were declining; and 22 (17 percent) were undetermined, largely because of the lack of available data resulting from sensitivity of the information or establishment of a new metric (see Table 3.2).

Culture and Personnel

Significant efforts have been made from the DIBP's leadership to signal commitment to the reform, build a single culture throughout the reorganised department, and support the workforce. Initial efforts included engaging employees, establishing a single uniform, combining management functions (e.g., human resources, finance, and badging), and standing up the ABF College, which demonstrated the leadership's commitment to the workforce and the reorganisation. However, efforts seemed to slow shortly after the reorganisation began, and the employee survey indicated significant dissatisfaction within the workforce, particularly with senior-leadership engage-

[1] GAO, *Department of Homeland Security: Progress Made and Work Remaining in Implementing Homeland Security Missions 10 Years After 9/11*, GAO 11 881, Washington, D.C., 7 September 2011.

Table 3.2
Operational Metrics Assessment

Outcomes	Budget (2015–20)[a]	Programmes: Total Measures (e.g., indicators)	Met Target or Improving	No Improvement	Did Not Meet Target or Declining	Undetermined[b]
Outcome 1: Protect Australia's sovereignty, security, and safety by managing its border, including managing the stay and departure of all noncitizens.		10	2	4	3	1
Programme 1.1: Border Enforcement		14	5	7	2	0
Programme 1.2: Border Management		25	11	4	1	9
Programme 1.3: Onshore Compliance and Detention (revised structure)		32	18	9	4	1
Programme 1.3: Compliance and Detention[c] (2015–16 structure)		0	–	–	–	–
Programme 1.4: IMA Onshore Management (2015–16 structure)		7	3	2	–	2
Programme 1.4: IMA Offshore Management[d]		0	–	–	–	–
Programme 1.5: Regional Cooperation		2	–	–	–	2
Unassigned metrics[e]	–	6	3	0	0	3
Outcome 1 totals		96	42	26	10	18
Outcome 2: Support a prosperous and inclusive society, and advance Australia's economic interests through the effective management of the visa and citizenship programmes and provision of refugee and humanitarian assistance.		3	1	1	–	1
Programme 2.1: Citizenship		2	–	1	–	1
Programme 2.2: Migration		14	14	–	–	–
Programme 2.3: Visas		8	4	1	3	–
Programme 2.4: Refugee and Humanitarian Assistance		2	2	–	–	–
Outcome 2 totals		29	21	3	3	2
Outcome 3: Advance Australia's economic interests through the facilitation of the trade of goods to and from Australia and the collection of border revenue.		0	–	–	–	–
Programme 3.1: Border-Revenue Collection		2	–	–	–	2
Programme 3.2: Trade Facilitation and Industry Engagement		3	1	0	2	0
Outcome 3 totals		5	1	0	2	2
Total for Outcomes 1, 2, and 3		130	64	29	15	22

[a] DIBP, *Portfolio Budget Statements 2016–17 Budget Related Paper No. 1.11: Immigration and Border Protection Portfolio; Budget Initiatives and Explanations of Appropriations Specified by Outcomes and Programs by Entity*, Canberra, 2016.

[b] The assessments in this table reflect examination of the 130 available metrics. Where possible, trends during the period 2014–2016 were identified. However, in some cases, the data were not available or the trends were not identifiable; in such cases, an assessment of "undetermined" was made. Additionally, given that data came from different sources, it was necessary to employ reasoned assumptions and professional judgments in making some of the comparisons.

[c] This includes elements of Programmes 1.3, 1.4, and 2.4 from fiscal year 2015–2016.

[d] This was Programme 1.5 in fiscal year 2015–2016.

[e] The term *unassigned metrics* refers to metrics that have not been identified as belonging to a particular outcome or programme.

ment. Overall, building a single culture and solving the personnel issues remains a work in progress. Continued senior-leader engagement will be central to making advances in this area.

Capability

Indicators of progress in building capability were seen in several key areas. The top line of the department reflected real savings, while the available data suggested that there was no negative impact on mission accomplishment. The DIBP also undertook efforts to build capacity in the planning, programming, requirement-generation, and budgeting functions of the department; although in the early stages, these efforts should improve the department's operational capacity across the DIBP mission space. Combining management functions was designed to result in greater support for the DIBP, as well as garner efficiencies. New equipment and technology had been recently incorporated into DIBP operations, but little data were available to assess whether these resources had yet resulted in either greater operational effectiveness or efficiencies. This question will likely need to be assessed after the capabilities have been in place longer and additional data are available.

Implementation of the Reorganisation Elements

Action Plan

The original action plan for integration was detailed, had high-level leadership emphasis, and established a framework for the integration. The reorganisation planning was carried out for approximately one year, resulting in a very detailed plan with objectives, milestones, and activities to be accomplished over the time horizon of the reorganisation. However, several shortfalls have been identified, which have negatively affected the implementation. The plan did not include adequate metrics that were defined and measurable. Furthermore, a detailed data-collection plan did not appear to be in place to track the key metrics. In short, the detailed planning in the pre-integration period did not follow through into execution. The placement of execution-monitoring with the first assistant secretary likely contributed to the loss of momentum, and the change to making the deputy secretary the responsible change agent was a strong move for both improving execution and signalling to the workforce. Interviews indicated that the operations orders for the integration were very detailed leading up to 1 July 2015, yet direction in the immediate aftermath was lacking. One individual noted that, in the absence of such direction, regional commanders were left to execute the integration without guidance in a decentralised manner.

Monitoring Progress

Achieving momentum for and monitoring the progress of the reorganisation required establishing a framework with proper metrics in sufficient detail to assess how well the organisation was performing over time. This was not explicitly accomplished prior to the integration and is being rectified with the development of new metrics, which are currently being evaluated by the DIBP for inclusion in reporting. These newly developed metrics will provide a standard set of data elements to be collected on a routine basis and included in a master database for further analysis, decision support, and (ultimately) resource allocation. Likewise, the incorporation of the Integration Action Tracker (an internal tracking document) will be important to sustaining momentum for the reorganisation, as will elevating the responsibility for reorganisation to the deputy secretary level.

However, several important shortfalls in the new metrics have been identified. First, they do not consider the full strategy-to-resources continuum.[2] The metrics are focused on operations, with little attention towards whether the department's strategic outcomes are being measured, assessed, or achieved. Therefore, even with the new metrics, assessing whether the overarching strategy of the DIBP is being realised will still likely not be possible.

Furthermore, with the nearly exclusive focus of operational issues, a variety of other important metrics associated with the health of the organisation, future planning considerations, resources and capabilities, and the continuing reform are not being adequately considered. Second, several areas such as refugee and humanitarian operations are not included in the current set of integration metrics, yet are key aspects of the DIBP mission.

Conclusions

Trends over the 2014–2016 period reflect that DIBP has been able to maintain the same level of productivity despite budget reductions, increased operational tempo, and the ongoing reorganisation. The integration of Customs and Immigration into a single department was a significant undertaking. Although evidence of a strong planning process leading up to the 1 July 2015 execution date can be seen, planning for execution-monitoring and assessment was problematic. Subsequent difficulties with a loss of momentum for the reorganisation were observed in the execution phase. This was also observed by the DIBP, and efforts are under way to rectify the situation.

In considering the progress the integration made between July 2015 and May 2016, the DIBP's development has been substantial. For example, in comparing the DIBP's integration with DHS's integration that has been ongoing since 2002, the operational and functional management integration of the DIBP appears to be more advanced in many areas. In the recent GAO report from which the assessment methodology was drawn, titled *Department of Homeland Security: Progress Made, but More*

---

[2] In the United States, the strategy-to-resources framework is best exemplified in the Department of Defense and includes the four pillars of planning, programming, budgeting, and execution, sometimes referred to as the *PPBE system*.

Work Remains in Strengthening Management Function,[3] the authors highlighted that progress had been made but that more needed to be done, even after well over a decade.

When considering one of the subordinate DHS organisations, U.S. Customs and Border Protection (with a similar mission to the DIBP), one sees evidence that the DIBP has already achieved equal or greater operational integration, cultural and personnel integration, and capability-building (including in planning, programming, requirement-generation, and budgeting functions), even after such a short period.

In looking to the future, the most-critical elements for progress in the reorganisation will be continued leadership engagement and the development of relevant metrics that describe the operational effectiveness and efficiency of the reorganised DIBP.

---

[3] GAO, *Department of Homeland Security: Progress Made, but More Work Remains in Strengthening Management Function*, Washington, D.C., GAO-15-388T, 26 February 2015.

CHAPTER FOUR

Conclusions

The report has focused on two overarching issues: the need for change in Australia's border management capability and how the integration has affected the operational effectiveness and efficiency of the newly formed DIBP.

The study identified the following conclusions:

- The transformation of the two organisations—Customs and Immigration—would have been required regardless of whether the integration of the two organisations had occurred.
  - Neither had demonstrated the effectiveness expected of a 21st-century border-management capacity for Australia.
  - Development of a 21st-century capability will depend on the professionalisation of the workforce and building the necessary organisational capacity.
- In assessing the operational effectiveness of this newly formed department during the period of 2014–2016, two overarching themes were the increased operational tempo and the ongoing reorganisation.
  - The DIBP has supported the government of Australia in the customs, immigration, and border-protection mission area during the period of 2014–2016, with no observable decrease in capability, while undergoing a significant reorganisation and a decrease in top-line funding.
  - A total of 130 operational programme performance measures were examined. The results indicate that 64 (49 percent) met targets or were improving, 29 (22 percent) remained constant, 15 (12 percent) did not meet targets or were declining, and the remainder could not be measured.
- The current integration of the DIBP began in July 2015, during which a comprehensive transformation was set in motion. This transformation envisioned more than just addressing identified shortfalls in a piecemeal manner; rather, there was a comprehensive reform which would be based on building the foundations for long-term growth in the organisation and workforce.
  - Given the leadership commitment and the capacity-building measures that have been established, such comprehensive reform is possible.

- However, immediately following the beginning of the integration, in July 2015, a loss of momentum occurred. Interviewees attributed the causes to a lack of post-integration planning, lack of organisational focus on the integration, and lack of consistent leadership engagement.
- The use of a system approach to completing the integration and subsequent reform will be important to ensuring that the comprehensive reform envisioned is achieved. This is especially important given that many of the shortfalls related to systemic failures.

The integration of the DIBP reflects an important inflection point in the history of customs, immigration, and border-management activities within the government of Australia. The degree to which this reform achieves its goals largely rests on the ability of the leadership to keep up the momentum, bring the workforce along, and ensure that the necessary capacities that have been built are able to survive.

ANNEX A

Assessment Plan: The Case for Change

Tasks

- What did the two organisations look like separately?
  - Identify strengths and weaknesses (these largely come out of the Australian Public Safety Commission capability reviews, and further evidence will be in documents such as the Palmer and Comrie reviews of Immigration and ACLEI reports on Customs).
- What has been done in the integrated organisation to harness the strengths of both former agencies? And to deal with the weaknesses of the two former organisations?
- Given that neither agency was achieving excellence separately, is the reorganised DIBP better positioned to do this as one department?

Methodology

1. Documentation.
   a. Catalogue documents. Examine the body of information and identify sources of information for the analysis.
   b. Develop a consolidated list of recommendations (and findings, where they exist) across the documents that have been provided.
2. Analyse trends and identify areas for detailed analysis.
   a. Identify areas of focus for more in-depth analysis.
      - Gain DIBP approval for the deep-dive areas. Intent will be to examine five areas in greater depth.
3. Conduct analysis using methods outlined above. Focus would be on addressing the questions identified in the tasks above. Expect that data analysis will require augmentation with interviews to clarify questions that arise and add context.
4. Develop set of overarching conclusions regarding the impact of the reorganisation.

ANNEX B

Interviews Conducted

Table B.1
List of Interviews Conducted

Name	Position
Rachel Noble, PSM	Deputy Secretary Policy Group (DIBP)
Michael Outram, APM	Deputy Commissioner Operations (ABF)
Michael Manthorpe, PSM	Deputy Secretary Visa & Citizenship Services Group (DIBP)
Cindy Briscoe	Deputy Commissioner Support (ABF)
Maria Fernandez	Deputy Secretary Intelligence and Capability Group (DIBP)
Jenet Connell	Deputy Secretary Strategic Reform Programme (DIBP)
Maree Bridger	First Assistant Secretary Executive Division (DIBP)
David Wilden	First Assistant Secretary Immigration and Citizenship Policy Division (DIBP)
Lachlan Colquhoun	First Assistant Secretary International Division (DIBP)
Linda Geddes	First Assistant Secretary Traveller Customs and Industry Policy Division (DIBP)
Clive Murray	A/g Deputy Commissioner Operations (ABF) Assistant Commissioner Strategic Border Command (ABF)
Stephen (Steve) Hayward	First Assistant Secretary Integrity, Security and Assurance Division (DIBP)
Ben Wright	First Assistant Secretary Corporate Services Division (DIBP)
Cameron Ashe	First Assistant Secretary Intelligence Division (DIBP)
Wayne Buchhorn	Assistant Commissioner Investigations Division (ABF)
James Watson	Commander Detention Operations Branch (ABF)
Tim Orton	Managing Director Nous Group

NOTE: PSM = Public Service Medal; APM = Australian Police Medal.

ANNEX C

Interview Questions

Questions for DIBP Interviews

Introduction

RAND had been asked to evaluate two areas. Interviews were employed to augment the official documents and other information provided to the study team.

First, RAND was asked to take a deeper and longer view of the two organisations as they existed, understand how the combined organisation has been able to incorporate into a single organisation, and assess the degree to which the new organisation has been able to mitigate weaknesses and reinforce strengths. For this phase, five areas were directed by the DIBP to be the focus of the analysis: (1) intelligence, (2) investigations, (3) detention, (4) integrity and corruption, and (5) learning and development.

Second, RAND was asked to evaluate the effectiveness of this newly formed department at the present by examining the data during the period of 2014–2016. This analysis focused on developing quantitatively informed trends during this period.

Questions

1. Biographical information
    a. Name and organisation: ____________________
    b. What was your position in the government?
    c. How long did you serve? What were your dates of service?
2. Pre-integration
    a. How was your organisation functioning prior to the integration?
    b. Was there a perceived rationale for the integration? If yes, what was it?
    c. Was the workforce in agreement with the need for change?
    d. Were appropriate resources allocated to the integration?
    e. Was pre-execution planning adequately done prior to the integration?
3. Post-integration
    a. What were the goals of the integration?
    b. What programmatic changes were intended to be implemented?
    c. Has the workforce been supportive of the implementation of the integration?

   d. What is your assessment of the degree to which the integration has achieved its stated goals and objectives?
   e. Assuming the goals and objectives have not yet been achieved, when do you assess they will be achieved?
   f. Is the organisation more capable today than prior to the integration?
   g. Are resources adequate for successfully conducting the integration?
4. Thoughts for the future
   a. What are the long-term prospects for building a professional customs, immigration, and border organisation?
   b. Other assessments concerning the reorganisation?
   c. Anything else you would like to add?

ANNEX D

Assessment Plan: Operational Effectiveness

Organisational Analysis

Using an objective, evidence-based analysis, how is the Department of Immigration and Border Protection currently performing?

It is now two years since the government announced its intention to integrate the ACBPS and the DIBP and ten months since the formal integration occurred on 1 July 2015. The analysis will examine how the integrated organisation is performing in the areas of

1. operational outputs
2. capacity outputs
3. people/workforce.

The elements of the framework have been divided into two categories, those directly related to organisational effectiveness and efficiency and those related to integration.

Questions have been developed in each category and are supported by data which includes the periods prior to the announcement of integration, the period where the agencies were integrating, and the current state of the integrated department.

Organisational Elements

1. Operational effectiveness and efficiency (demonstrated sustained progress)
    a. What are the trends in operational effectiveness and efficiency during the period of 2014–2016?
    b. To what degree have the stated objectives been accomplished over the past two years?
    c. What efficiencies have been incorporated into the new organisation?
2. Capability
    a. What organisational changes have occurred during the period 2014–2016 (e.g., aligned functions)?

   b. What has been the effect on capability across the organisation during the period of 2014–2016?
   c. Have adequate resources been devoted to achieving outcomes for government?
   d. To what degree has the organisation integrated management and administrative functions (e.g., services, IT, badging, procurement, financial, human capital)?
3. Culture and personnel (leadership commitment)
   a. What is the degree to which the integration has been accepted within the workforce?
   b. Has there been appropriate (and adequate) communication with the workforce?
   c. Have there been any effects on talent management (positive or negative)?
   d. Has the department and ABF brand gained acceptance?
   e. Has the leadership demonstrated commitment to the effort?

Integration

1. Objectives (action plan)
   a. What were the objectives for the integration of Customs with the DIBP?
   b. Was there an action plan for the integration? If so, how well (i.e., close to the published schedule and effectively) has the plan been executed?
2. Monitoring progress (framework to monitor progress)
   a. How has the department been monitoring the progress of the reorganisation?

ANNEX E

Detailed Findings from Assessing Operational Effectiveness as a Result of the Reorganisation

The information in this annex corresponds to the five assessment categories in the GAO report: operational effectiveness and efficiency, capability, cultural and personnel, action plan, and monitoring progress. This annex includes additional information and assessments pertaining to these categories.

Operational Effectiveness and Efficiency

This annex includes a background section with several roll-up charts providing information on the DIBP performance, with focus on the 2014–2016 period. These charts support high-level comparisons of workloads to assess whether there have been any early impacts as a result of the reorganisation. These data are not intended to be comprehensive descriptions of the mission space but rather used in supporting the assessments that have been made. Also included in the annex are the operational assessments of the performance of the DIBP according to three specified outcomes (see below).

Background

The following charts demonstrate the overall trends regarding border management and enforcement. Overall, Australia has experienced significant increases in border-related activities in personnel arrivals, imports, and vessels (Figures E.1–E.3, respectively). The arrival of goods has increased in recent years. Each of these movements creates an increased workload and requires a decision, verification, and potentially an inspection by DIBP organisations and personnel.

Examples by Outcome and Programme

Outcome 1: Protect Australia's sovereignty, security, and safety by managing its border, including managing the stay and departure of all noncitizens.

Regarding illegal activities and border enforcement, no clear trends are evident across the different subset of metrics presented in Table E.1. Anomalies such as the major drug seizure in quarter 1 of 2015 reflect a single large seizure that occurred.

Figure E.1
Historical Overview of Visitors and Residents Arriving from Overseas Locations

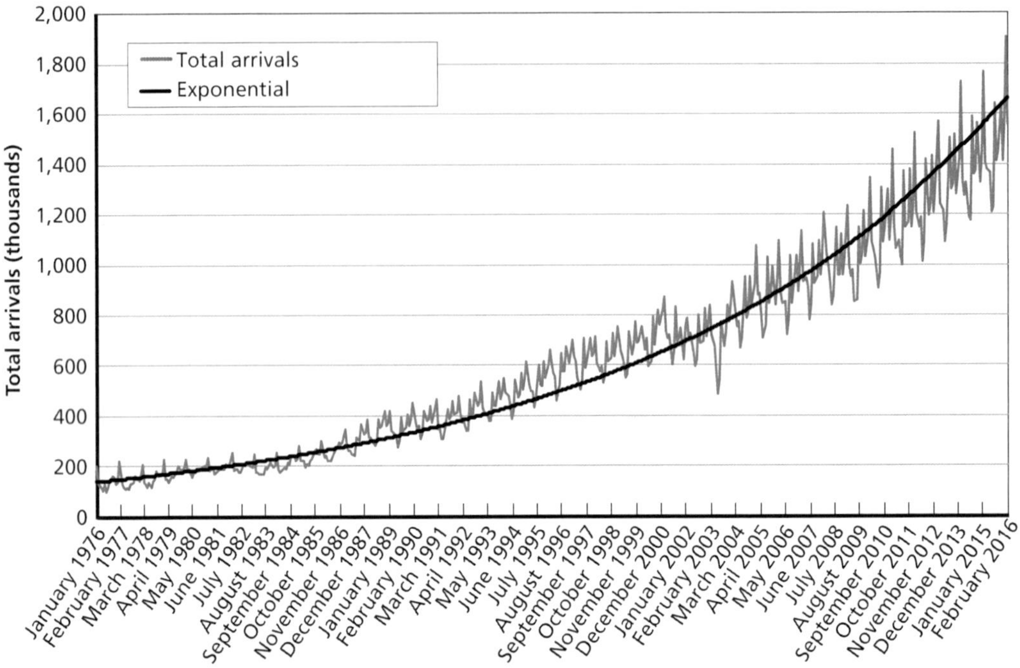

SOURCE: Australian Bureau of Statistics, "3401.0—Overseas Arrivals and Departures, Australia, Feb 2016," web page, 5 May 2016, Table 1.
RAND *RR1713-E.1*

Table E.1
Categories of Border Infractions

Category	2014, Quarter 4	2015, Quarter 1	2015, Quarter 2	2015, Quarter 3	2015, Quarter 4	2016, Quarter 1
Illegal-worker warning notice issued	65	384	123	72	163	62
Weight of major drugs and precursors (kg)	557.94	4,033.33	1,053.23	584.00	1,442.10	1,469.90
Passenger and crews refused immigration clearance	1,482	585	964	806	802	771
Number of detections of undeclared firearms	306	805	495	34	578	368
Number of visa cancellations	4,283	12,806	16,687	12,106	14,212	12,608

SOURCE: Data provided by the DIBP.

Figure E.2
Historical Overview of Goods Imported, by Value

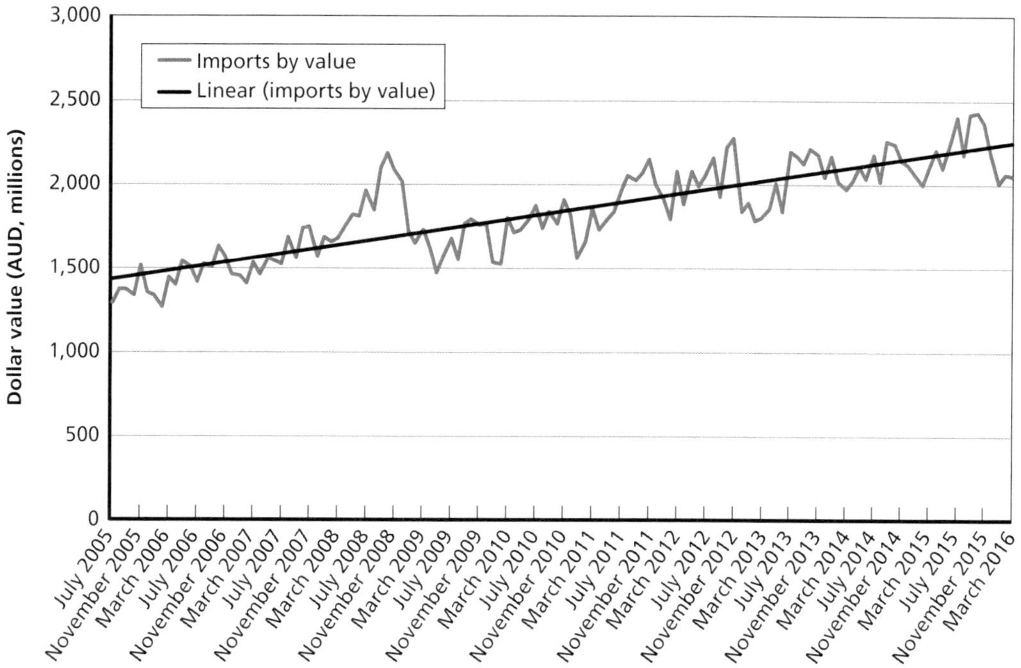

SOURCE: Australian Bureau of Statistics, "5368.0—International Trade in Goods and Services, Australia, Mar 2016," web page, 1 June 2016, Table 35a.
RAND *RR1713-E.2*

The overall trends noted for processing illegal immigrants and overstayers (people becoming unlawful) indicate mixed developments across the mission space. For example, onshore and offshore IMAs have seen a reduction over time, which is positive, while the numbers of overstayers and unlawful noncitizens have remained approximately constant in the 2015–2016 period. However, in looking at longer trends in the last two metrics, one observes that the number of overstayers since 2010–2011 is going down, while the estimate of unlawful noncitizens is increasing.

- For IMAs (onshore and offshore), the data display a decreasing trend, indicating that fewer people are being held in these facilities and therefore the costs for these facilities are decreasing, which is a positive outcome (Programmes 1.3–1.4) (see Figure E.4).
- The number of illegal overstayers has remained relatively constant over the past fiscal years (see Table E.2).
- The number of unlawful citizens is consistently increasing, which is a negative trend (see Table E.3).

Figure E.3
Historical Overview of International Arrivals of Vessels Carrying Goods or Passengers

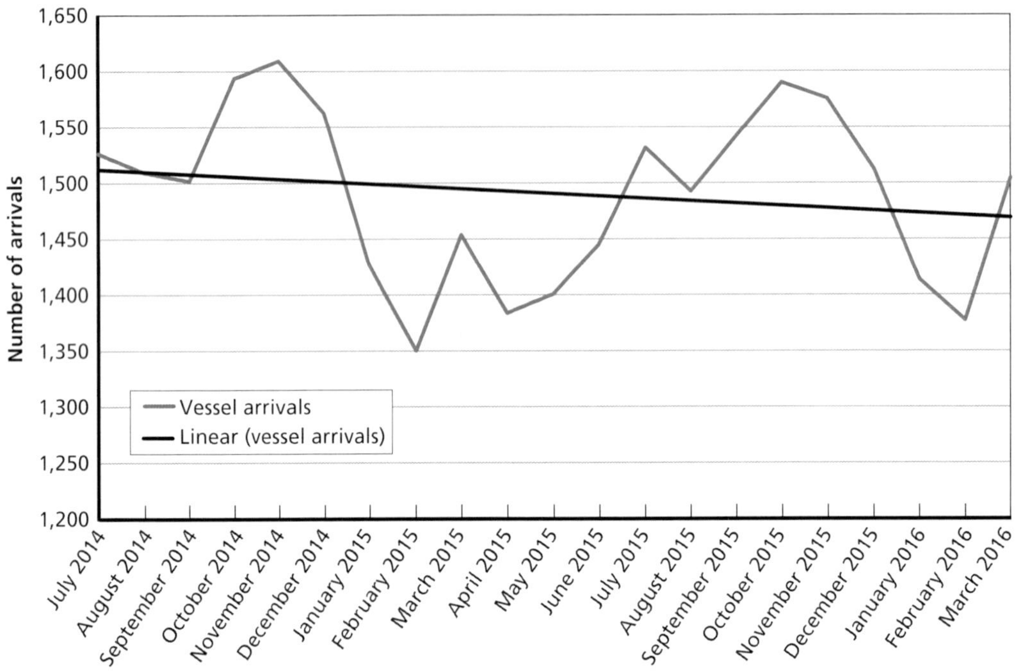

SOURCE: Border data provided by the DIBP.
RAND *RR1713-E.3*

Table E.2
Overstayer Statistics

Outcome 1	2010–2011	2011–2012	2012–2013	2013–2014	2014–2015	2015–2016 (estimate)
Overstayers	19,570	19,540	16,460	14,940	13,750	14,467

SOURCE: Data provided by the DIBP.

Table E.3
Estimate of Unlawful Citizens

Outcome 1	2010	2011	2012	2013	2014	2015
Estimate of unlawful noncitizens[a]	53,900	58,400	60,900	62,700	62,100	62,000

SOURCE: Data provided by the DIBP.
[a] Estimated as of 30 June of each year.

Figure E.4
IMAs and Non-IMAs (Onshore and Offshore)

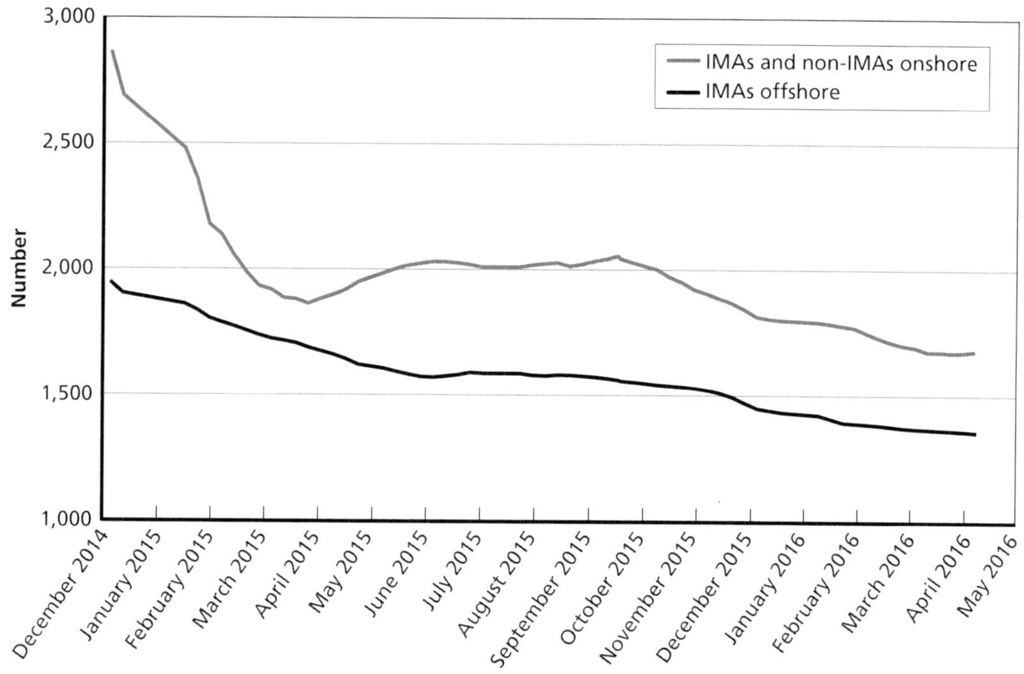

SOURCE: Data provided by the DIBP.
RAND *RR1713-E.4*

Outcome 2: Support a prosperous and inclusive society and advance Australia's economic interests through the effective management of the visa and citizenship programmes and the provision of refugee and humanitarian assistance.

Data associated with this outcome reflect that there is little change in the citizen or visa application areas in terms of percentage within standards (processing time in days) (see Tables E.4 and E.5).

- However, in considering the number of citizen applications, there is an approximate 15-percent reduction from 2013–2014 to 2015–2016 (estimated).
- For the temporary-visa application process, during the period of 2013–2014 to 2015–2016 (estimated), there was approximately a 17-percent increase (see Table E.5).

Outcome 3: Advance Australia's economic interests through the facilitation of the trade of goods to and from Australia and the collection of border revenue.

Revenues for visas and customs are continuing to steadily increase. These are an increasingly important source of revenue for the government of Australia (see Table E.6).

Table E.4
DIBP Citizen Application Throughput

Outcome 2	2013–2014	2014–2015[a]	2015–2016 (estimate)
Percentage within service standard	74.8	82.9	79.6
Total applications	192,085	189,887	162,925

SOURCE: Citizenship data provided by the DIBP.

[a] On 1 July 2014 the service standard changed from 60 to 80 days.

Table E.5
DIBP Temporary-Visa Application Throughput

Outcome 2	2013–2014	2014–2015	2015–2016[a]
Percentage within service standard[a]	89.0	88.1	88.4
Total applications	1,688,073	1,750,716	1,979,067

SOURCE: Temporary-visa data provided by the DIBP.

[a] As of 31 March 2016.

Table E.6
Revenues Administered by the Government

Outcome 3	2013–2014	2014–2015	2015–2016	2016–2017 (estimated)
Revenues administered by the government (AUD)	12.0 billion	14.0 billion	16.7 billion	17.5 billion

SOURCE: Border revenue data provided by the DIBP.

Capability

This section examines departmental-level capabilities, which include such areas as improving the department's processes, budgets (and revenues), material expenditures (and modernisation of equipment), personnel, and training.

The development of the 2016 *Strategy Handbook* demonstrates a commitment to build capacity in the planning, programming, requirement-generation, and budgeting functions of the department.[1] This newly published document is intended to be a foundation for these efforts. The handbook is described in the section titled "How to Use This Handbook," as the "first time an enterprise-level publication has been developed

[1] DIBP, *Strategy Handbook*, Canberra, March 2016.

to explain the capability management process for the Department of Immigration and Border Protection (the Department)."

Beginning with the elemental step of defining the term *capability*, the handbook goes on to describe how various processes, such as intelligence and identity; decisions on trade, travel, and immigration; and enforcement activities must be developed within the DIBP mission space. The DIBP expenses categorised by outcome (Figure E.5) highlight that expenditures are decreasing from 2015 to 2020. The largest decrease is expected from 2016–2017 to 2017–2018. The consistent reductions reflect the inclusion of efficiency measures resulting from the reorganisation.

Although the expenses are decreasing, the revenues in the reorganised DIBP are anticipated to increase from 2014–2015 to 2019–2020 by more than 40 percent as a result of increased trade and travel (Figure E.6). Note that this information was also presented in tabular format under the Outcome 3 area.

The DIBP staffing levels are also decreasing in comparison with the 2012–2013 high point (Figure E.7). For the 2014–2015 and 2015–2016 periods, the personnel totals remained relatively constant. Although Figure E.7 depicts an increase for 2016–2017, this does not reflect the planned 480-personnel decrease in staffing by the end of 2020 as a result of the reorganisation.

Using head-count data, changes to organisations with more than 100 personnel were calculated. Over the period of analysis (fiscal years 2013–2014 to 2015–2016),

Figure E.5
DIBP Expenses Categorised by Outcome

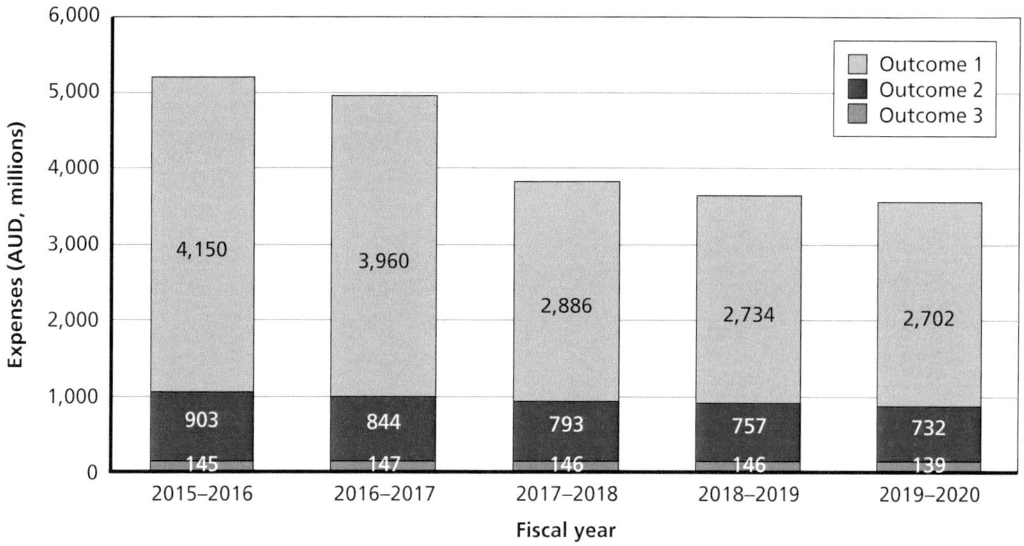

SOURCE: DIBP, *Portfolio Budget Statements 2016–17 Budget Related Paper No. 1.11: Immigration and Border Protection Portfolio; Budget Initiatives and Explanations of Appropriations Specified by Outcomes and Programs by Entity*, Canberra, 2016.

RAND *RR1713-E.5*

Figure E.6
Revenues Administered on Behalf of the Government

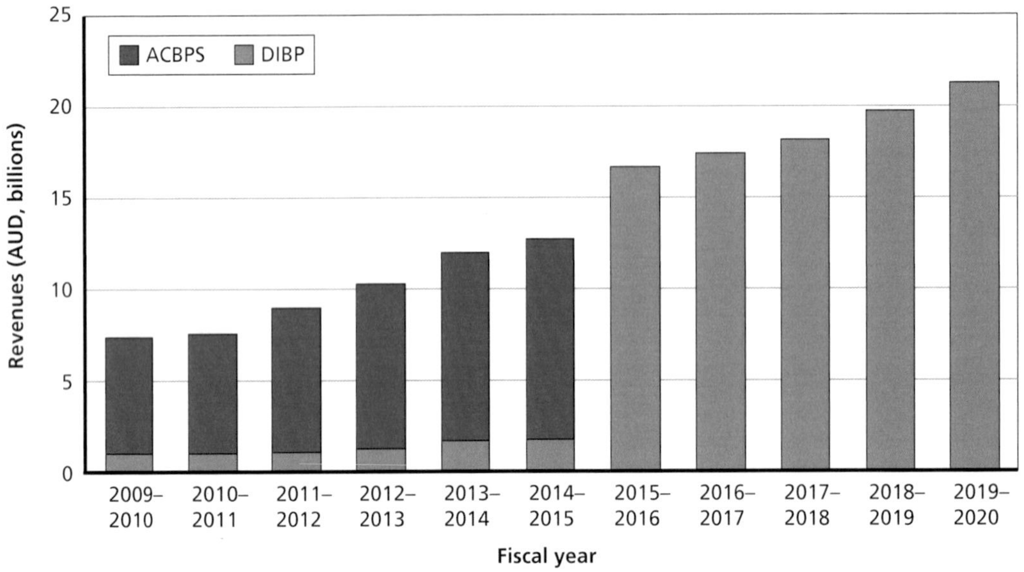

SOURCE: Financial data provided by the DIBP.
RAND *RR1713-E.6*

Figure E.7
DIBP (and ACBPS) Staffing Levels (Average)

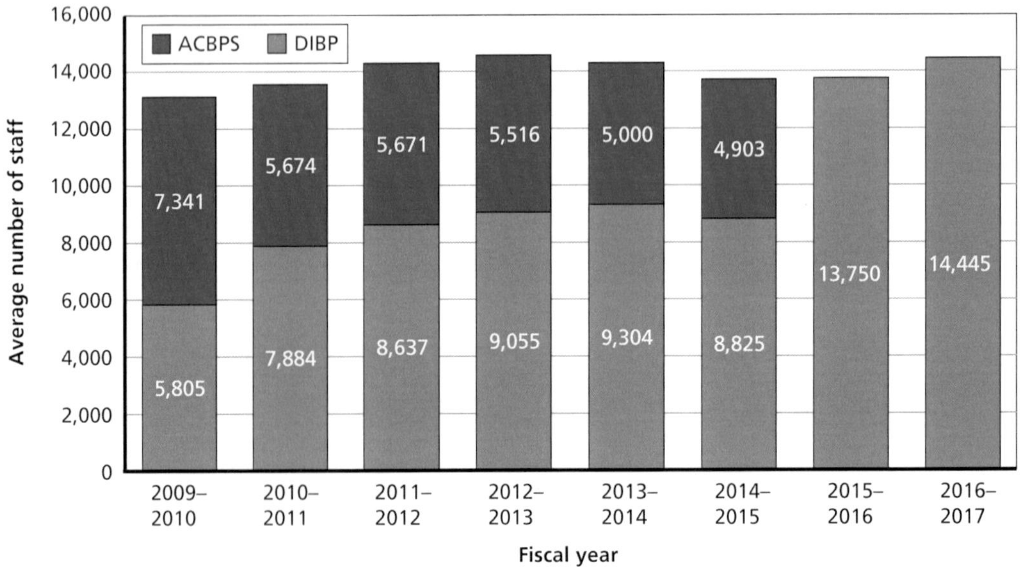

SOURCE: DIBP personnel summary.
RAND *RR1713-E.7*

the total staffing level of the combined Immigration and Customs organisations grew slightly (0.7 percent), from 13,923 to 14,025 (as of 30 April 2016). As expected, many of the support divisions (people, IT, finance, and policy) shrank as a result of the integration. Many of the operational divisions (Strategic Border Command, Visa and Citizenship Management, and Investigations) stayed at roughly the same levels or grew slightly.

The data indicate that, within organisations, significant turbulence is occurring. Undoubtedly, these changes are causing stress and uncertainty within the workforce. The fact that DIBP effectiveness and efficiency, as measured by the increased operational tempo, is occurring at the same time as the major staff reorganisation is also a likely factor in workforce issues.

Table E.7 provides detailed overviews of the gains and losses for large organisational elements.[2]

The new organisation is intended to "generate significant savings and provide the 'optimal structure' to pursue a more effective approach to border protection."[3] This expressed intent implies an organisation with increased operational effectiveness and efficiency of border operations and the direct requirement to increase or build a greater overall capacity.

One such change that has been incorporated is the development of the ABF College, which was designed to improve the training and education of the workforce. The infusion of new technology, such as a biometrics tool announced in September 2015, is yet another example of building greater capacity to manage borders, for legitimate trade and travel and for border-security purposes.

The combining of human resources, finance, and badging, for example, likewise demonstrates an enhanced capacity with respect to the management functions critical to successful operations. These integrations are expected to save fiscal resources and will also allow DIBP leadership to better manage these resources.

The development of a combined IT footprint has the potential for further efficiencies and greater organisational capacity, although this has not yet been accomplished. The efficiency would result from savings from eliminating the IT management organisation organic to Customs. The increased capacity would result from increased information-sharing and eliminating an unnecessary IT seam between the former two departments' IT sections.

The development of cross-functional teams, combining the immigration, customs, and border functions within lower-level organisations, also serves as a potentially important new capability for the DIBP and ABF. However, the degree to which these cross-functional teams will be successful will need to be evaluated over time. One

---

[2] *Large* was defined as those organisations larger than 100 staff over the period of analysis.

[3] National Commission of Audit, *Towards Responsible Government: Phase One*, Canberra: Commonwealth of Australia, February 2014.

Table E.7
Gains and Losses for Large Organisations (i.e., More Than 100 Personnel)

Organisation	Fiscal Year			Percentage Gain/Loss
	2013–2014	2014–2015	2015–2016	
Border Management	253	341	398	57.3
Border Force Capability	653	744	926	41.8
International Division	118	162	152	28.8
Refugee & Humanitarian Visa Management	507	590	616	21.5
Community Protection	798	819	893	11.9
Legal	247	273	276	11.7
Identity & Biometrics	159	155	170	6.9
Integrity Security & Assurance	175	189	187	6.9
Intelligence Division	369	381	393	6.5
Strategic Policy & Planning	148	154	155	4.7
Major Capability	361	380	371	2.8
Digital Transformation & Channels	458	479	465	1.5
Visa & Citizenship Management	2,115	2,195	2,129	0.7
Strategic Border Command	3,777	3,597	3,780	0.1
Investigations	388	348	368	–5.2
Executive Division	240	210	227	–5.4
Corporate Services	338	335	312	–7.7
People Division	398	426	366	–8.0
ICT Division	787	711	674	–14.4
Traveller Customs & Industry Policy	220	188	181	–17.7
Finance Division	261	245	214	–18.0
Immigration & Citizenship Policy	209	155	168	–19.6
Detention Services	179	147	141	–21.2
Children Community & Settlement	361	342	282	–21.9

SOURCE: DIBP personnel summary.

NOTE: Gray rows = ABF.

concern regarding these teams is training. Little evidence exists (outside of the ABF College curriculum) that these cross-functional teams are receiving specialised training that could be useful in operational settings. It is also not clear the degree to which the intent is to make the immigration, customs, and border specialists within a team interchangeable, which would likely require additional training and changes to authorities.

In addition, several categories of enhancements in business process and capability were identified. The categories included border force, future traveller, trusted trader, case management, data intelligence, mail modernisation, and infrastructure. They encompassed a broad range of activities, from development and fielding of new equipment to increased information-sharing.

A draft document titled *Transformation Investments and Business Impacts* also highlighted planned spending from 2015 to 2019, presented in Table E.8.[4] The projected spending reflects anticipated resourcing plans that had been developed for enhancing the operational capacity of the combined DIBP.

Culture and Personnel

Culture and personnel issues were factored into the planning for the reorganisation from the outset. A workforce communications plans was a centrepiece of the employee engagement planning. A series of events and outreach activities were conducted in an effort to explain the reorganisation to the workforce. During the pre-integration period and immediately thereafter, senior departmental leaders made public speeches on the importance of the reorganisation, highlighting national objectives as a key impetus for the change.

Important tangible efforts to build a single culture across the newly formed department included combining management functions, such as human resources, finances, and badging, as discussed previously. Developing a single uniform for the

Table E.8
Investment and Business Impacts

Category	Resources, 2015–2019 (AUD)
Visa	215 million
Border clearance	245 million
Compliance and enforcement	333 million
Intelligence	184 million
Workforce and corporate	123 million

SOURCE: Data provided by the DIBP.

---

[4] DIBP, *Transformation Investments and Business Impacts*, Version 0.2, Canberra, 8 March 2015.

ABF rather than having separate customs, immigration, and border-protection attire was also significant. Although perhaps seemingly minor initiatives, these efforts were critical to signalling to the workforce that they were part of a new organisation, with a new brand and a newly emerging DIBP culture.

The establishment of the ABF College provides another example of building a new culture for the organisation. Such branding might be considered to be a secondary outcome to the primary goal of education and training provided to college attendees, but it serves as an important public demonstration of the leadership commitment to the organisation and to building a common culture.

Public communications, which consistently include pictures of the secretary and commissioner, likewise serve as important signals to the newly formed organisation, providing outward evidence of both continuity and change. A variety of internal communications with staff have also been provided: news articles on the intranet home page, all-staff emails, *The Week Ahead* (a weekly all-staff bulletin), *Together We're Talking* (a monthly managers' bulletin), *Border Bulletin*, posters, and screensavers, to name a few.[5]

The reorganisation included building cross-functional teams that brought customs, immigration, and border personnel together at the lowest levels. This too became an important signal to the organisation and helped to build a unified culture even at these lower tactical levels. Such teams can also have benefits in operational effectiveness and efficiency.

Although many early efforts to build a unified DIBP culture and support the workforce during the transitional period were put in place, data suggest that not all of these efforts were successful. Shortfalls were identified in several areas.

- The perceived lack of senior-leader communications during the execution period has been observed as requiring additional emphasis. Other specific concerns were a lack of department-level feedback on the status of ongoing initiatives and the employee-survey results.[6] More on this will be discussed below.
- The employee survey indicated that dissatisfaction and even some disenfranchisement existed within the workforce. Generally, the employees expressed great support for their missions, their own efforts, and their immediate supervisors, while expressing dissatisfaction with senior departmental leadership. Of note, these findings are consistent with those from the DHS ratings from the employee surveys across the U.S. government conducted over the past several years.[7] In assessing the meaning of the results, one must consider that employee surveys tend to be trailing-edge indicators demonstrating that it is easier to change organisations

---

5 Internal and corporate communication, Department of Immigration and Border Protection, undated.

6 Internal and corporate communication, Department of Immigration and Border Protection, undated.

7 Beth Cobert, "OPM Releases Full FEVS Report for 2015," Office of Personnel Management, 6 October 2015.

than people's perceptions and sentiments. It also demonstrates why leaders must communicate with the workforce and explain key decisions.

- Senior-leader engagement has been identified as an area for increased emphasis. Major criticisms include the following:
  - The DIBP leadership has been perceived as being too "Canberra-centric."
  - Senior leaders have been seen to be disengaged from their staff.
  - There is a perceived failure to highlight the important work of the department across the government, with stakeholders, and with the Australian public.
- Concerning the departmental-level culture, two areas of concern were identified. Despite early efforts to build one organisation, recognition exists that there is no one single department-level identity yet. Finally, a perception exists that the department is too risk-averse.

Action Plan

An efficiency measure recommended by the National Commission of Audit in 2013 was "to merge the border control functions of the Department of Immigration and Border Protection (DIBP) and the Australian Customs and Border Protection Service (Customs) into a 'single, integrated border agency.'"[8] The commission's recommendation was based on two anticipated outcomes, "the potential to generate significant savings and provide the 'optimal structure' to pursue a more effective approach to border protection through 'a series of integrated activities both beyond and within the border.'"[9] Based on these stated goals and analysis which identified the potential for AUD 480.5 million savings over four years and the elimination of 480 full-time positions (or 3.4 percent), the efficiency measure was approved.

For approximately one year, the integration planning was carried out, resulting in a very detailed plan with objectives, milestones, and activities to be accomplished over the time horizon of the integration. A Gantt-chart format was employed, which is a common method of recording the planning and execution process.

However, early in the action-plan development and following through in execution, some key elements were not established that would have aided the successful transition. RAND's analysis identified notable shortfalls.

- Key areas were not captured in two categories, missions and strategic-level outcomes:

[8] National Commission of Audit, *Towards Responsible Government: Phase One*, Canberra: Commonwealth of Australia, February 2014, pp. 207–208.

[9] National Commission of Audit, *Towards Responsible Government: Phase One*, Canberra: Commonwealth of Australia, February 2014, pp. 207–208.

  - Missions: Several areas that are part of the DIBP mission space have not been addressed. For example, cybersecurity represents a technology area that will be critical to maintaining immigration, customs, and border operations and protecting personal private information but is not represented in the action plan. Procedures for protecting against invasive species, although the responsibility of the Department of Agriculture and Water Resources, is an area where the DIBP provides important support yet has not been included. Countering violent extremism is another example of an area not explicitly addressed, although it is implied in the operational metrics that have been developed. A final example of an area not explicitly considered in the action plan is interagency (i.e., cross-government) collaboration and information-sharing.
  - Strategic-level outcomes: The action plan concentrates heavily on operational issues while not deliberately considering strategic-level outcomes. Details on this issue will be discussed below, in the section on monitoring progress.
- Lack of metrics: The plan did not include an articulation of detailed metrics necessary to monitor and characterise the progress made towards accomplishing the objectives of the reorganisation. More on this will be discussed in the following section, on monitoring progress, but, in short, such an omission prevented assessing whether the high-level objectives that served as the rationale for the reorganisation, as well as the reorganisation action plan's objectives, were achieved. This shortfall was recognised, and metrics have been developed for many of the key functions; the use of the metrics has not been incorporated into the DIBP to date, although they are expected to be once approved.
- Stalled progress shortly after implementation: Available documentation provided by the DIBP, as well as information that RAND found through open sources, indicated that the relatively fast start in implementation eventually slowed, and the reorganisation floundered. This identified lack of progress over a six-month period resulted in the development of a more formal execution plan that included changing the reporting chain and the visibility of the implementation progress, the development of detailed metrics for capturing operational data, and greater emphasis on evaluating operational effectiveness and efficiency.
- Leadership's visibility of the plan execution: Initially, responsibility for monitoring the execution of the reorganisation rested with a first assistant secretary. While this is a high position within the DIBP, it lacked the authority to synchronise and direct the entire department; this is best managed one level up—by a deputy secretary of DIBP. The shortfall in positioning the responsibility for reorganisation has also been identified, and an appropriate shift in responsibility has ensued. Additionally, a new entity—the Strategic Reform Group, under the direction of a deputy secretary—has been established for the purpose of monitoring reorganisation implementation. This reflects another positive change, which should increase the momentum of the reorganisation.

- Loss of momentum potentially resulting from lack of leadership communication: A lack of execution information about the implementation being disseminated to the workforce was observed, which likely contributed to a loss of momentum. Although the employee-engagement newsletter, *Portfolio News*, was provided to the workforce for this purpose, pointed communications concerning the reorganisation progress appear to have diminished.

Monitoring Progress

Achieving momentum for and monitoring the progress of the reorganisation required the establishment of a framework with proper metrics in sufficient detail to assess how well the organisation was performing. This was not explicitly accomplished prior to the reorganisation and is being rectified using the Boston Consulting Group–developed metrics that are currently being evaluated for inclusion within DIBP reporting.

These newly developed metrics will provide a standard set of data elements to be collected on a routine basis and included in a master database for further analysis, decision support, and ultimately resource allocation.

Additionally, given the implementation issues discovered shortly after integration was initiated on 1 July 2015, the DIBP has instituted the Integration Action Tracker, specifically to monitor integration. The first of these trackers is dated March–July 2016 and was rolled out on 21 March 2016.

Although it appears that efforts are under way to ensure that a framework will be in place for improving the monitoring of reorganisation implementation, some shortfalls continue to be observed:

- Lacks a systems approach to metrics: Examining metrics using a systems approach allows for considering a particular aspect of the mission space within context.
  - One cannot draw conclusions based on such statistics as "number of firearms confiscated" without understanding the context for the data element. Did the number go up or down based on an increase or decrease in the number of patrols? Were technology solutions or targeting algorithms employed which increased the probability of making detections?
  - Employing a systems approach to border metrics for the firearm example above would entail identifying the relevant components that compose the seizure of firearms, determining the relationships between them, and assessing how they have changed during the time horizon under consideration. Only armed with such detail can the cause and effects be appropriately linked and the system fully understood.

- Assessing strategic outcomes: The current 20 measures of success developed by the Boston Consulting Group[10]—referred to as the "measures of success"—are largely operational metrics, and as such do not consider the full strategy-to-resources continuum.
  - None of the 20 measures is related to strategic outcomes. In fact, only three of the 20 measures examine anything other than operational issues.
    - Two of the 20 measures (number 14, "staff satisfaction ratings on access to information," and number 19, "integration of workforce and culture") are directly related to the integration.
    - One metric (number 13, "effectiveness in procuring key resources") pertains directly to resourcing or capacity-building issues.
  - As none of the measures being developed can be considered to be strategic, assessing strategic outcomes will likely be problematic. Furthermore, with such measures, assessing whether the overarching strategy of the DIBP is being achieved will also likely not be possible.
  - With the nearly exclusive focus on operational issues, a variety of other important metrics associated with the health of the organisation, planning considerations, resources and capabilities, and the continuing reorganisation are not being adequately considered.
- Metrics not all-inclusive: The current group of metrics developed by the Boston Consulting Group is not complete in several regards.
  - Operational versus reorganisation focus: In the long term, such an operationally focused list might be appropriate; however, given the expressed desire to monitor the progress of the reorganisation, it is likely not adequate.
  - Operational areas not addressed. As examples, the refugee and humanitarian mission areas have not been considered in the metrics. This shortfall has been noted by the DIBP. Other areas not included are cybersecurity, invasive species, and interagency collaboration (including information-sharing).
- Data availability and formatting are incomplete.
  - In looking at the data through the lens of an "input-process-output-outcome" model, the data provided were largely either inputs, such as dollars expended or personnel totals, or outputs, such as interdictions made. Little data were available regarding the internal processes or the outcomes of an activity, so few conclusions could be drawn regarding operational effectiveness and efficiency in some key areas.
  - Additionally, a large majority of the data provided by DIBP came from reports or preestablished formats (such as the operational reports) and not in the form of data sets consisting of raw data. In these report formats, certain assump-

---

[10] Boston Consulting Group, *Reform and Integration: Measures of Success—Final Deliverables from Strategic Advisor Phase 1*, briefing, December 2015.

tions have likely been made, which, unless annotated, were not available to the RAND team. Complicating the analysis was that the data structures (e.g., program definitions, metrics, and data collected) changed during the period under scrutiny, making longitudinal comparisons difficult for some metrics.

  - In considering the issue of the operational effectiveness and efficiency of the DIBP or the status of the reorganisation, having well-defined metrics that are linked to strategic and operational outcomes—expressed as objectives, milestones, and activities—becomes essential. Merely measuring statistics will not allow for understanding the DIBP's organisational processes, determining whether they are functioning in an optimal manner, or making analytically informed policy and resourcing decisions.
- Rolling up metrics should be consistent.
  - Exhaustive lists of individual metrics can be time-consuming for staff and leadership to analyse and present for decisions. To make the metrics more useful and with fewer requirements for post-collection processing, a standard list of reports will likely prove useful.

Abbreviations

ABF	Australian Border Force
ACBPS	Australian Customs and Border Protection Service
ACLEI	Australian Commission for Law Enforcement Integrity
AGSVA	Australian Government Security Vetting Agency
APM	Australian Police Medal
DHS	U.S. Department of Homeland Security
DIAC	Department of Immigration and Citizenship
DIBP	Department of Immigration and Border Protection
GAO	U.S. Government Accountability Office
IMA	illegal maritime arrival
IT	information technology
OSA	Organisational Suitability Assessment
PSM	Public Service Medal

References

Assistant Secretary Australian Border Force College, *Report to Accompany BFORT Course Schedule*, Canberra: Australian Border Security, undated.

Australian Border Force, *L&D and ABF College Board SUBMISSION—Learning Governance Model*, Canberra: Department of Immigration and Border Protection, 17 March 2016.

Australian Bureau of Statistics, "3401.0—Overseas Arrivals and Departures, Australia, Feb 2016," web page, 5 May 2016, Table 1. As of 29 August 2016: http://www.abs.gov.au/AUSSTATS/abs@.nsf/allprimarymainfeatures/C5503B4DA1C9BC2FCA257FAA0019EACC?opendocument

———, "5368.0—International Trade in Goods and Services, Australia, Mar 2016," web page, 1 June 2016, Table 35a. As of 29 August 2016: http://www.abs.gov.au/AUSSTATS/abs@.nsf/allprimarymainfeatures/36027E4332A7011FCA257FC50017E16E?opendocument

Australian Commission for Law Enforcement Integrity, *Operation Heritage—A Joint Investigation of Alleged Corrupt Conduct Among Officers of the Australian Customs and Border Protection Service at Sydney International Airport (Interim Report)*, Canberra, February 2013. As of 29 August 2016: https://www.aclei.gov.au/sites/g/files/net846/f/report022013-operationheritageinterimreport.pdf?v=1455097900

———, *Operation MYRRH—An Investigation into "Private" Illicit Drug Use by Certain Australian Customs and Border Protection Service Officers*, Canberra: Commonwealth of Australia, January 2014.

———, *Operation Heritage (Final Report)—A Joint Investigation of Alleged Corrupt Conduct Among Officers of the Australian Customs and Border Protection Service at Sydney International Airport*, Canberra, February 2014.

Australian Customs and Border Protection, *Australian Border Force Bulletin #3*, Canberra, March 2015.

Australian government, *The Integrated Business Model Must Do's: Transforming the Compliance, Case Management and Detention Business*, Canberra, 25 September 2007.

———, *Customs Reform Board, First Report*, Canberra: Commonwealth of Australia, June 2013.

———, *Learning and Development, ABF Recruit Training*, Canberra, December 2014.

———, *Building One Organisation—Pulse Check Findings Summary*, Canberra, July 2015.

Australian Public Service Commission, "Security," in *Foundations of Government*, Canberra, 23 May 2012. As of 29 August 2016: http://www.apsc.gov.au/publications-and-media/archive/publications-archive/foundations-of-governance/chapter-13-security

———, *Capability Review Action Plan: Australian Customs and Border Protection Service*, Canberra, 2013.

Bergin, Anthony, *A Safer Australia: Meeting the Challenges of Homeland Security*, Barton: Australian Strategic Policy Institute, 30 Janaury 2009. As of 29 August 2016: https://www.aspi.org.au/publications/a-safer-australia-meeting-the-challenges-of-homeland-security-by-anthony-bergin/Policy_Analysis36.pdf

Boston Consulting Group, *Reform and Integration: Measures of Success—Final Deliverables from Strategic Advisor Phase 1*, briefing, December 2015.

Cobert, Beth, "OPM Releases Full FEVS Report for 2015," Office of Personnel Management, 6 October 2015. As of 29 August 2016: https://www.opm.gov/blogs/Director/2015/10/6/OPM-Releases-Full-FEVS-Report-for-2015/

Comrie, Neil, *Inquiry into the Circumstances of the Vivian Alvarez Matter*, Canberra: Commonwealth Ombudsman, September 2005.

Department of Immigration and Border Protection, *Department of Immigration and Border Protection: Machinery of Government Changes*, Canberra, undated. As of 31 August 2016: https://www.anao.gov.au/work/performance-audit/department-immigration-and-border-protection-machinery-government-changes

———, *MIR Summary—Nauru Review by Philip Moss*, Canberra, undated.

———, *Agenda Item 6.5: Tabling of Management Initiated Reviews (MIR); MIR Summary, Review by KPMG of Financial Audit of the Community Assistance Support (CAS) and Asylum Seeker Assistance Scheme (ASAS) Service Providers*, Canberra, 2013–2014.

———, *The Learning and Development Strategic Plan*, Canberra, July 2014.

———, *Review of Onshore Detention Facilities Maintenance and Asset Management*, Canberra, October 2014.

———, *Transformation Investments and Business Impacts*, Version 0.2, Canberra, 8 March 2015.

———, *Health Check of Quality Assurance Across the Department*, Canberra, April 2015.

———, *Employment Suitability and Security Screening*, Canberra, 29 June 2015.

———, *Integrity Measures*, Canberra, 29 June 2015.

———, *Professional Standards*, Canberra, 29 June 2015.

———, *Visa Decision Maker Vocational Training Pathway Training Needs Analysis*, Canberra: Commonwealth of Australia, 2015.

———, *Strategy Handbook*, Canberra, March 2016.

———, *L&D Quality Assurance Procedural Instruction*, Canberra, 7 April 2016.

———, *Deputies Committee Brief: Learning and Development Strategic Plan*, Canberra, 20 May 2016.

———, *Leadership Framework*, Canberra, May 2016.

———, *Capability and Competency Project: Project Overview*, Canberra, 2016.

———, *Capability and Competency Project: Vocational Competency Profile*, Canberra, 2016

———, *Portfolio Budget Statements 2016–17 Budget Related Paper No. 1.11: Immigration and Border Protection Portfolio; Budget Initiatives and Explanations of Appropriations Specified by Outcomes and Programs by Entity*, Canberra, 2016. As of 29 August 2016: https://www.border.gov.au/ReportsandPublications/Documents/budget/2016-17-pbs-full.pdf

———, *Vocational Competency Profile: Intelligence Analyst*, Canberra, 2016.

———, *Vocational Competency Profile: Intelligence Technologist*, Canberra, 2016.

———, *Vocational Competency Profile: Investigations Compliance and Regulation, Border Force*, Canberra, 2016.

Department of Immigration and Citizenship, *The DIAC Strategic Plan 2010–11: A Strategic Plan to Build Stronger Migration and Visa Services*, Canberra, 2010.

———, *Strategic Plan 2011–12*, Canberra, 1 July 2011.

Department of the Prime Minister and Cabinet, *Martin Place Siege: Joint Commonwealth—New South Wales Review*, State of New South Wales, January 2015.

DIAC—*See* Department of Immigration and Citizenship.

DIBP—*See* Department of Immigration and Border Protection.

GAO—*See* U.S. Government Accountability Office.

Lee, Jane, and Nick McKenzie, "Immigration Officer Warns on Risk to National Security," *Sydney Morning Herald*, 6 August 2014. As of 29 August 2016:
http://www.smh.com.au/federal-politics/political-news/immigration-officer-warns-on-risk-to-national-security-20140806-3d8yy.html#ixzz4Df0blfIz

National Commission of Audit, *Towards Responsible Government: Phase One*, Canberra: Commonwealth of Australia, February 2014. As of 29 August 2016:
http://www.ncoa.gov.au/report/docs/phase_one_report.pdf

Palmer, Mick, *Inquiry into the Circumstances of the Immigration Detention of Cornelia Rau*, Canberra: Commonwealth of Australia, July 2005. As of 29 August 2016:
http://www.border.gov.au/ReportsandPublications/Documents/reviews-and-inquiries/palmer-report.pdf

Queensland Organised Crime Commission of Inquiry, *Submission by the Australian Commission for Law Enforcement Integrity, Canberra: Australian Commission for Law Enforcement Integrity*, 7 July 2015.

Rudd, Kevin, "National Security Statement," speech to the House of Representatives, Canberra, 4 December 2008. As of 29 August 2016:
http://parlinfo.aph.gov.au/parlInfo/genpdf/chamber/hansardr/2008-12-04/0045/hansard_frag.pdf;fileType=application%2Fpdf

U.S. Government Accountability Office, *Department of Homeland Security: Progress Made and Work Remaining in Implementing Homeland Security Missions 10 Years After 9/11*, GAO 11 881, Washington, D.C., 7 September 2011.

———, *Department of Homeland Security: Progress Made, but More Work Remains in Strengthening Management Function*, Washington, D.C., GAO-15-388T, 26 February 2015.